12/95

The Way
of the
Spirit

The Wisdom
of the
Ancient Nanina

The WAY of the SPIRIT

The Wisdom of the Ancient Nanina
by Billy Whiskers

ACS Publications
San Diego, CA

Cover and illustrations by Maria Kay Simms
Author Photo by Mark S. Harris

International Standard Book Number
0-935127-10-0

Published by ACS Publications, Inc.
PO Box 34487
San Diego, CA 92163

Manufactured in the United States of America

Contents

INTRODUCTION

I am Nan; a word which means a person apart. The very concept of a loner was bewildering to the people I remember; the gentle Nanina. It was to them as though a foot were to live and walk about without being attached to a body.

Yet, strangely, I must be Nan in order to properly remember them, for a memory three thousand years old can stand few distractions.

A beautiful, wise and gentle people with a natural grace which the world hungers for today. I see their dust blow past my eyes in the wind and know that their legacy is a memory in one mind alone. This must not be!

So I now give their memory into your keeping. Do with it as you will but remember the Nanina.

I weep as I write these words but not for the Nanina, for their lives were full and their days were joyful. They were *ishtahei,* (like a stone), and complete in a way that the world has forgotten. Their lives poured forth from their very souls and the words of their souls were uttered by their mortal mouths.

Modern man, not even sure that he has a soul, can only stand in awe of these people, who understood that their soul was not something dangling loosely somewhere like a family heirloom; grandpa's gold watch perhaps, or great Grandma's cameo brooch. Their very lives were their souls' expression in physical existence.

Listen now to the tales of the Nanina. Listen, and if you are wise enough, change your lives. Make them full and joyful. Learn to live your soul.

FIRST CONTACT

Some years ago I found myself driving across New Mexico on my way from San Diego to Oklahoma.

As I neared the high plains, I felt the urge to turn off onto a small road. Checking the highway atlas I saw that a series of country roads would lead me in the right direction. I told myself that I was bored with the easy but monotonous interstate highway I had been traveling. Ah, how we twist and stretch to make the promptings of our soul fit the practical, no-nonsense attitude of modern humanity. Now I need no such excuses. This much at least have the Nanina taught me.

After over fifty miles of travel with no sign of a town, or even sight of a house, and with my gas gauge too close to empty for comfort, I came into a small settlement consisting of one gas station, a dusty store and perhaps a dozen houses. Gratefully I filled my tank. I bought a loaf of bread, some lunch meat, and filled my Thermos with coffee. There was a three-stool lunch counter where I could have had a bowl of that wonderful New Mexico chili, but something prompted me to stop somewhere and eat at the side of the road. Had I ignored those urges, my life would not have taken the turn that it has.

A few miles from town I found a picnic table, seemingly set up in the middle of nowhere.

As I turned off the engine, the silence struck me with a shock. No birds sang or flew in the sky. No horses or cattle cropped the short buffalo grass. The sigh of the ever-present high-plains wind accentuated rather than broke the silence.

A strange prickling sensation made the hair on my arms stand up, but I reassured myself that it was only the unaccustomed desolation.

As I sat at the table eating, I read the inevitable graffiti carved and scratched into the tabletop— "Paco 78," "Harry and Alice were here"—the common person's one pathetic shot at immortality.

Sipping the last of my coffee, I looked about me. As far as the eye could see were low rolling hills: bare brown earth with here and there a dusting of gray-green buffalo grass. In the depressions between the hills, deep gullies had been gouged into the earth by the infrequent but violent rains. Most of them terminated in shallow depressions crusted with the salt and alkali left behind when the thirsty wind and sun sucked out the water.

I twisted the top onto my Thermos and got to my feet. Suddenly dizzy, I grasped the edge of the table for support. I heard the Thermos thud to the ground. Everything seemed dim and hazy, as though the sun were suddenly setting. I seemed unable to focus on anything. I remember thinking, "Oh great! I'm about to pass out and there hasn't been a car by since I got here."

Children laughing? Dogs barking? Was I hallucinating? Then, as my vision cleared, I thought I was losing my mind.

The harsh, dry wind had turned gentle, carrying the fragrance of lush growth. I was standing in waist-high grass, some sort of grain. All around me the hills were covered in vegetation, waving in the breeze like a verdant sea. Brooks bubbled in the tiny valleys between the hills, marked by bands of trees along their banks. The parched depressions had become ponds and small lakes, flashing and sparkling in the sun.

Scattered about these ponds in groups of three to half a dozen were rounded huts made of willow hoops and thatched with grass. The nearest group was at the foot of the hill on which I stood. Each hut had its own neatly swept hearth of stone. Some were in use, and wisps of smoke rose from these as women dressed only in short leather skirts knelt cooking. Men and women squatted here and there talking and laughing, and around and between them in splendid confusion ran laughing children and barking dogs.

Never have I seen skin the tone of theirs. Not the coppery brown of the Indian nor the lighter brown of the Oriental and certainly not the color of the deeply tanned white. These people had skin that could only be called golden. I thought, incongruously, that this was the tone the "beautiful people" tried so hard for but never quite achieved. The hair of these golden people ranged in color from dark brown to almost blond.

As I stood there in wonder and bewilderment, my eyes were drawn to one man in particular. Medium in height, he wore only a loincloth and leather headband to keep his shoulder-length hair under control. All in all, he appeared no different from any of the others.

Storyteller (how did I know his name?) kept the oral history of his tribe in his head and at night entertained any who cared to come to his hearth with stories both traditional and made up on the spot (how did I know that?).

As I looked, he stood up and turned toward me, palm uplifted in greeting. With a shock I realized that even as I looked at him with my eyes, somehow I was also seeing myself through his.

Then I was standing, grasping the gouged tabletop and staring at a salt pan full of alkali— the bare bones of what moments before had been a lake.

Most of the rest of that day I sat there, my thoughts buzzing like gnats— never quite lighting, just going around in aimless circles. I remember the rueful thought that whatever the store put in that coffee, it could bring a fortune in the right market.

Eventually I pushed the experience to the back of my mind, as we will with things we don't understand, and in time it became a sort of secret treasure to be taken out and dusted off occasionally, then packed carefully away again.

When the sun sank low, I resumed my trip to Oklahoma to visit my sister. Soon after I arrived I found myself looking at land for sale, something I had not been considering (at least consciously).

"Well," I thought, "I suppose my wife can join me when the house is up. My son is grown and happily married and I have a small income from my Navy retirement." I supposed I had as much right to be a middle-aged crazy as the next man. So I ended up the proud owner of forty acres of Goat's Bluff in the eastern hills of Oklahoma.

My conscious plan was to grow my own food on some cleared land and become one of the growing number of self-sufficient modern homesteaders, but it soon became apparent that more was going on here than I had bargained for.

The first year was given over to clearing land, pulling stumps and, with the help of my nephew, getting a start on a timber-framed house.

Halfway down the steep north slope of my ridge is an outcropping of sandstone, and I found myself drawn there often to sit and daydream. I know now the importance the Nanina place on dreaming, but at the time it simply seemed a good place to relax. Often I thought of my experience in New Mexico and wondered what it meant.

There is a natural seat on the stone and it seems to have the peculiar property of easing aches and pains with what I had presumed was its stored solar heat. As I sat there one day easing a back aching from pulling stumps, my thoughts turned to Storyteller and that peculiar double vision. Almost immediately I felt a jolt where my back rested against the stone, as though I had touched a bare electric wire; but there is no electricity anywhere near the north slope.

In the same instant a voice spoke loudly. I am certain that the voice was in my ears and not in my mind. The words were strange and had no meaning for me at the time.

"*Nanina ishtahei.*" I had heard my first words in the language of the Nanina—a language that had not been heard on Earth in three thousand years, though I did not know that then.

Now I had two experiences to worry over, and I chewed at them like a dog with an old bone.

Weeks went by with no further happenings. On the one hand I was relieved, but on the other I had the feeling that I was like a man in quicksand whose only way out was to go farther in, hoping to feel solid ground under his feet.

Then one day, as I was working in my new fields, I heard the voice again, this time less dramatically for I knew that it came from somewhere in the recesses of my own mind. It was Storyteller's voice, this time in strangely accented English. "The people are like stone." I knew this was a translation of "*Nanina ishtahei,*" and I also knew, don't ask how, that it signified, "The people are one."

This knowing without knowing how I know was strange to me at the time. It became more frequent, though never commonplace, as time went on.

One more word the voice spoke: "**Remember.**" And now it is my task to remember so that you may remember. **Remember** the Nanina.

KNOW YOUR SOUL

These are tales told at the hearthstones of Storyteller. How do I know? I know because I remember. I remember as you would remember something that happened when you were very young.

When I feel the memories stirring, I put pen to paper and write them as I remember them, never knowing how the stories will end and often not even what the next word will be.

His stories mean whatever they mean to you. In the Nanina manner, he leaves room between the lines for you to fill in; but to hear them properly, you must learn, as I did, to know what you know without knowing how you know.

Creation

You are eternal. Before time was, you were. When time ends, you still shall be. You were with the Creator at the beginning of time, dancing with joy and clapping your hands in delight as the shiny new toy came into being: Our Mother the Earth, *Hiyei Hiyasu*, Mother of All.

Your spiritual hands helped the Creator to draw up the hills and mountains just so and placed the grass and trees to clothe and beautify her body.

Your spiritual fingers poked into the earth here and there and traced the lines that ran between the hills, and water filled them and flowed. You scooped out great depressions and the water flowed into them and became the sea.

Then the Creator taught you to draw water from the sea and put it into the sky as clouds, and to make the air move as wind to move the clouds about so that the water would fall on the grass and trees and flow into the rivers, ponds and lakes, and they would run forever; and the Earth and her children would have food and drink.

All of these things came out of your soul and knew themselves and knew their source; and *Hiyei Hiyasu*, Mother of All, was alive and bore children. Fish swam in the water and birds flew in the air. Animals walked the surface of the Earth; and even deep within the Earth was life; and it knew itself and found joy in its being.

And you, engrossed in your new plaything, drew closer and closer until a part of your soul grew flesh and became physical; and the Earth, which you helped to create, gave you birth.

The larger part of your soul remained with and in the Creator and now looks out through your physical eyes as you walk and create in flesh and matter.

As a child playing in the sand forgets itself in the patterns it is creating with shells and shiny pebbles, so do you forget yourself in the patterns of your physical existence.

But the child will soon enough remember. Then it will abandon its playthings and turn homeward till tomorrow's play brings new patterns and new delights.

I tell you now. **Remember**. Return to your soul for it is who you are.

Before commenting, let me set up the "ground rules." It would be tedious indeed to preface every remark with "The Nanina believe" or "I think," therefore I will state each thing as fact. Whether you accept it as such or only as something to think about is entirely up to you. Let me, however, ask you not to think it to death. Just sort of try it on for size. See if it feels right. Learn to know what you know without knowing how you know.

Your soul is not only immortal in the future, as many of us have always believed, but in both directions. You not only always **will be**, but always **were**. Your soul exists **within** the Creator and always has. Your soul, and thus you, are a very real part of the Creator's being. We are immortal indeed!

Then what do we (in the sense the word is usually used) represent? We are the eyes and ears of the Creator in the physical world. Our task is to create in flesh and matter, thereby adding to the being of the Creator, for he becomes ever greater and will never cease growing.[1]

We need have no fear of being destroyed by the Creator at some hypothetical end of the world or swallowed up, thereby losing our individuality, for we always were and will always be, even after the end of time.

Time itself (at least as we know it) was a creation to make physical existence easier to handle. Imagine trying to juggle past, present and future with all their myriad choices, actions, joys and sorrows in some eternal now and you will see the necessity for "our" time.

The physical earth was not created out of thin air like some magic trick, but constructed **through** us out of our collective souls (which, don't forget, are made of the Creator's very being). It seems somehow fitting that the Earth, which was to be our home, was constructed of our very substance. The Earth, thus made physical, in turn gave birth to the bodies which we wear, so that we may directly experience physical reality rather than being merely observers. If we are to create in flesh and matter, it follows that we must **be** flesh during our time here.

Everything that we see is essentially a part of our souls made physical and therefore sentient, aware of itself and its source— us. The idea that the Earth is alive has recently been accepted by many people, not a few of whom are scientists.

How are we to determine the truth or falsity of these ideas? We

---

[1] The Creator is neither male nor female but a perfect balance of both. Separation of the sexes was adopted as one of the laws of physical reality and does not exist in the spiritual realm.

I find, however, that the English language has no personal pronoun to express this other than **it**, which I find completely inappropriate. Reluctantly, I have followed tradition and use the masculine **he**.

already **do** know. We have only to remember by temporarily removing our attention from our physical surroundings and returning to the knowledge of our own soul. I do not refer to faith but to **knowing** because we remember.

For elaboration on these ideas, read Storyteller's next tale.

Awareness

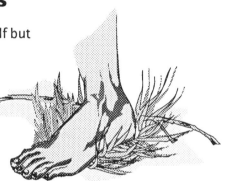

The foot walks. It knows itself but it does not know why it walks or where it walks. It knows the earth on which it walks, but only the part where it presently stands. It knows that it sometimes steps high but it does not know why. It is unaware of the branch lying on the ground which it steps over. It turns this way and that but it knows nothing of the rocks and bushes it walks around. It bears a burden but does not know that this burden is the body of which it is a part. It is good to walk and that is enough. It walks to the hearthstones.

The hand reaches out for the food lying on the hearth. It knows nothing of food and does not know how it came to the hearth or why it reaches out. It is good to reach out and pick up. That is enough.

The mouth tastes the food with its tongue and chews it with its teeth. It knows nothing of the foot which brought it here or the hand which placed the food within it. It does not know where the food came from or where it goes when it is swallowed. It is good to taste and chew and that is enough.

The eye sees all these things but does not know how it sees or what the things it sees mean. It sees the branches and rocks but cannot direct the foot around them. It sees the food but cannot direct the hand to pick it up and place it in the mouth. It is good to see. That is enough.

The mind feels the earth under the foot and sees the obstacles before it. It tells the foot to step over and walk around. It sees the food and knows what it is. It tells the hand to reach out. It tastes the food with the tongue and chews it with the teeth. It knows where the food goes and why it eats that food. It knows all these things but—somehow—it is not enough.

For when the foot rests and the tongue lies softly in the bed of the mouth, when the hand lies gently on the thigh of your beloved and all your body lies on the soft, fragrant grass of your bed, the mind does not rest. It looks this way and that, seeking something more.

Like a coyote on the trail of a rabbit, it twists and turns this way and that, in and out of the bushes of its thoughts; and as it seeks, the very object of its search walks softly behind it whispering, "I am here, I am here."

I tell you now. Turn the eyes of your mind away from the branch and the hearth. See not the foot or the hand or the mouth. Turn and look within. Look into the eyes of your soul, for it is you.

The words in these tales are the words I remember at the hearthstones of Storyteller. They are not my words— or are they? How can I remember when I was not there— or was I? Like Storyteller, I leave space between the lines of my thoughts. Fill it in as you will.

One word however is my own and that is the title, for Storyteller's tales have no titles of their own. If you do not approve my choices, feel free to substitute your own.

Remember that these tales are oral because the Nanina had no written language. Tribal history and genealogy were carried in the head of the Storyteller. "Storyteller" served as both name and title and there was a new one each generation.

Being oral, the tales are meant for the ear. Read them aloud. Try getting a few friends or family members together. I think you will enjoy them better that way. Use your own gestures and vocal effects. Storyteller will approve. They were meant to be passed on in that way.

The previous tale pointed out some of the problems of physical perceptions. The following tale warns of the interpretation of those perceptions in the mind.

Shadows

The man looks into the bushes and sees a rabbit. Slowly, so as not to startle it, he reaches for the throwing stick tucked into his loincloth. With a snap of the arm and wrist, he throws. His aim is true and he steps over and picks up—a stone!

His sister looks into a pond and deep within it sees a fish. She eases her hand gently into the water, fingers widely spread. Quick as she can, she grasps and lifts from the water—a leaf!

They return home and around the hearth that night they tell of the magic rabbit that turned to stone and the fish that became a leaf.

The people touch the stone and lift the leaf and murmur in wonder.

But the stone was always a stone, and the leaf was blown into the pond by the wind.

The eyes saw truly, and only in the mind did the stone become a rabbit and the leaf a fish.

The eyes look and see a piece of wood, sinew and a bundle of reeds. The mind looks through the eyes and says, "Ah, a bow and a bundle of fine arrows."

But the bow **is** wood. Is it really a bow—or part of a tree? Is the sinew really a bowstring—or part of a deer's leg? Are the reeds arrows—or the stems of water plants?

And **is** the tree really just a tree? Is it not a part of the earth on which it stands? Is the earth part of the sky through which it moves? Is the sky part of—**what**?

So the eyes of the soul see and perceive truly, but the mind makes what they see into something else. As the hunter wishes to see a rabbit, and his sister a fish, so the mind wishes to see what can be touched by the hands.

But the hands can touch only the tree. They cannot touch the soul of the tree, and so the mind pretends it is not there—and yet it is.

The eyes of your soul perceive the soul of the tree and know it as a part of itself since the beginning of time.

It is good to look outward and see the physical world, but it is sometimes good to look inward and see with the eyes of the soul.

I tell you now: unless you sometimes turn your eyes inward, you will see stones as rabbits and leaves as fish.

We are constantly told to stop daydreaming and see things as they really are. If we take this advice, however, we will find ourselves seeing only a small part, the physical part, of things. Since the physical is only temporary and the spiritual eternal, I leave it to you to judge what is real.

The tendency to try to translate spiritual truths into physical terms is an all-too-human failing. We must learn that even as our physical eyes have a spiritual counterpart, so does our physical mind, operating through the brain, have a spiritual counterpart operating through the soul. Few of us have any experience in its use, but perhaps it is time we learned.

Logic will serve you very well in the everyday world and I certainly am not telling you to abandon it. You will find, however, that if you try to use it in matters of the soul, it will lead you so far astray that you will, as in the tale, see stones as rabbits and leaves as fish.

Try phrasing spiritual questions very strongly. Direct the questions inward with all the emotion you can muster. Then dismiss it from your mind. In the midst of your everyday activity, you will suddenly **know**. If you are alert to it, this sort of direct knowledge will often come to you even when you are not aware that you have sought it.

Trust such knowledge. It may have an immediate application in physical life, then again it may be *"whishta hei"* knowledge (cloud-like). *Wishtahei* knowledge will, when you try to translate it with the part of your mind devoted to everyday activity, change shape. Twisting and turning, constantly showing different faces, wisps of it drifting here and there, it will be as difficult to translate as it would be to grasp a cloud. Play with it if you wish. Our spiritual activity needs much more playfulness in it. Don't fret. Your spiritual mind knows well what to do with it and will, insofar as possible, translate the parts of it that are useful to the physical mind.

Please allow me a personal observation here. Whenever someone presents an idea to me about which I am doubtful, I apply the acid test. Make a joke about it. If it puffs up like a toad, and appears pompous and indignant, stick a pin in it and cast it aside. The deflated idea is useless at best and harmful at its worst. I am firmly convinced that the Creator loves a joke. His being grows in our joy and laughter.

Be forever alert, however, not to use humor as a weapon to hurt others. Punch someone's nose and it will heal. Harm someone's sense of worth or pride in self and you may well warp their lives.

The Nanina always took care, especially in the case of children, not to harm another's pride. This next tale illustrates this.

Trails

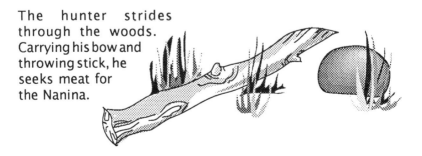

The hunter strides through the woods. Carrying his bow and throwing stick, he seeks meat for the Nanina.

As he goes, he leaves directions for those who follow so that he may be found. He places one stone atop another: go straight ahead. He lays a stick on the ground with a stone on one end, pointing right or left. He lays a stone on the ground near a stream with a line of pebbles pointing straight, or right, or left, meaning cross, or wade up- or downstream. He leaves other signs meaning "I have seen deer" or "I have taken a rabbit." The trail is plain to those who know how to read it.

After a few days his brother follows, carrying a packboard, rope and sharp stone knives so that he may help carry out what the hunter has taken.

He takes two boys of the Nanina with him, so that he can instruct them in the ways of the hunter. The boys carry their first real bows and arrows.

As they walk, he points out the trail markers and explains how to interpret them, but the boys are busily searching the bushes with their eyes. They dream of their pride if they are able to bring meat to the Nanina people, and so their ears do not hear him.

The man knows this, for he is not too old to remember his first trip to the wooded hills. He remembers what was done then and knows what he must do now.

The man walks more quickly, still instructing and pretending that he thinks they listen. The boys, who were close by him, are now behind and his voice grows dimmer as they lag.

Suddenly they realize they can no longer see or hear him. They do not know where he is; and with fright, they realize that they do not know where they are.

The man watches to keep them from harm, but they do not know this.

No longer feeling like mighty hunters, they thrash about in the brush, scratching their arms and legs in thickets and falling over logs.

As it begins to grow dark, they huddle in the shelter of an overhanging rock, their chins trembling and tears in their eyes.

The man has no wish to hurt their pride and so he steps into the open, pretending that he thinks they have been with him all along.

"Ah," he says, "You have found a fine camping place for the night. Gather some dry wood and we will soon have toasted grain and nuts for supper."

The next day the boys walk close by him, paying close attention to his teaching. By the time they reach the hunter, they are good indeed at reading trail signs and know the ways of finding their way home from the wooded hills.

So is there a well-marked trail through the wooded hills of your soul, but distracted by your physical existence, you step over the markers and never see them. Again and again your soul instructs you in their use, until its voice grows dim and you find yourself lost and alone; but you are never really alone, for your soul watches to keep you from harm.

I tell you now. Live your life in joyful fulfillment, but do not neglect the trail of your soul.

Your soul and the Creator allow full choice of your goals in physical life. This freedom must be if we are to be fully creative in this existence. Once a goal is chosen by you as a physical self, your soul will mark the best trail to follow in order to attain that goal without harm to yourself or others.

By not paying attention to these trail markers we constantly wander astray. What are these trail markers we have been missing? They are simply the innate knowledge always available to us. The sudden **knowing** that we all too often talk ourselves out of because we cannot back it up with worldly logic. In time, this habitual ignoring becomes so ingrained that we are no longer aware of receiving it.

Whenever we wander so far astray that we cannot find the trail at all, the soul simply lays out a new one starting with where we now are. Thus it is always possible to attain a goal as there is always a fresh trail before us.

Until we learn to utilize the knowledge of the soul, we must suffer the consequences of our wrong choices. **Please do not confuse this with punishment or burden yourself with guilt**. There are simply problems that will inherently follow a wrong choice.

Your task must be to blend your physical perceptions with your spiritual insights.

If you are still uncertain of the relationship between the physical you, the spiritual you (your soul) and the Creator, consider this next tale.

Perceptions

The fish swims in the lake. It breathes the water in and out. The water flows over its body as it moves. It leaps and splashes with joy and the water rejoices with it.

The bird flies in the air. Its wings move up and down and the air carries it as it flies. It breathes the air in and breathes it out as a song of joy. The air rejoices in the song.

The deer runs on the ground. It feels the ground as its hooves pound against it. It feeds on the brush which grows in the ground. It prances in joy. The ground shares the joy with it.

The water moves in and out of the fish as it breathes, but only a tiny part of the lake moves in and out.

The air carries the bird as it flies, but only a tiny part caresses the bird's wings.

The ground feels the pounding of the deer's hooves, but only a tiny part of it trembles.

Yet, though only a small part of our mother acts upon her children, they provide perception for *Hiyei Hiyasu*, Mother of All, the Earth. Without them, she would be unable to perceive her physical being.

The creatures of the Earth are a part of her. Without her, they would have no existence, and without them, she would have no reason to be.

You create wonderful things with your hands. Even more wonderful things are created by your mind. You find joy in these things, and through your eyes, and hearts and minds, your soul rejoices with you.

Only a small part of the water, the air and the ground embraces her children, yet the whole Earth is aware of them as a part of her, and she as a part of them. So only a small part of your soul touches your mind and heart, and yet through this part your entire soul is aware of you as a part of it and it as a part of you.

And when the Creator made your soul, it was made of the Creator's being. The Creator is aware of your soul—and you—and rejoices with your soul—and with you—and splashes with the fish, and sings with the bird, and prances with the deer, and the Creator's being grows in the joy of his creations.

I tell you now. Without the Creator you would have no existence—but without you, he would have no reason to be.

This tale ends with a rather startling idea, but give it a chance. Let's examine it. The essential nature of the Creator is creation. One of these creations is the physical reality which was created through us and which we inhabit. Without us, the Creator would have no perception of this very real part of his being and it would tumble into chaos. The same is true of other individualized selves in other realities. His existence and growth depend to a very real degree on our own existence as a part of him.

The Nanina Creator, who needs you as much as you need him, says, "Sing, laugh and dance. Eat the food of the earth and savor its delights. Watch the sparkle of sun on water, see the splendor of sunsets and let your eyes rejoice. Hear the songs of the birds and feast with your ears. Use your minds and create with your hands, and at night share the joy of your body with your beloved, for I am with you and rejoice and savor and share all of this as a part of you."

I like this perception of God far better, and find it far more reasonable than the God most modern people worship, if they worship at all. A God who does not really need us, but keeps us as a sort of pet. Only his infinite patience keeps him from squashing us like a bug. (And in many congregations he is expected to do just that at a last judgment.) A God who says, "Turn your eyes from worldly things. Sing my praises or feel my wrath. One wrong move and Hellfire for all eternity."

Make your choice. I've already made mine.

WHO IS STORYTELLER
—What Does He Represent?

When Storyteller first appeared in my memory, I was dismayed and somewhat confused. Instinctively I knew that there was much potential for knowledge here and that no harm would come of it— and yet—

There are old tales of demons who come bearing gifts that at first seem wonderful. Little by little the prey are seduced until they begin to lose control of their lives— and sometimes of their minds and souls. According to these tales, the demon never lets up till either you or it is triumphant once and for all.

Long ago I had thought through these tales and come to the conclusion that these situations are brought about by misperceptions of their own spiritual activity by the "possessed."

New spiritual knowledge comes to them which is beyond the dogma of whatever religion they follow. Rather than expand their spiritual horizons, they try to cram it into the old mold, which is too small to contain it. The spiritual information which was once true and relevant becomes distorted till it bears little resemblance to the original message.

The leftover energy is then attributed to a demon, or nowadays perhaps to a being from outer space. Such a warped outlook can lead to all sorts of problems.

In light of my experiences, however, I decided to reexamine these beliefs. It seemed prudent, before going any further, to determine whether or not I could control these phenomena.

When memories began to stir, I deliberately turned my thoughts elsewhere. Immediately the memories ceased and did not return till I had relaxed my mind and bade them enter. Numerous times I tested and the results were always the same. Several times I stopped them for weeks. It seemed I was in full control, at least on my end.

When the tales would resume, they would start where they had left off, as though there had been no break. I could sense Storyteller's gentle chuckle. He well knew what I was doing. If this was a demon, it was a singularly good-natured one.

Storyteller certainly came bearing gifts, but they were not worldly ones. He offered me no power over others, no riches, eternal youth, fame or beautiful women. What he offered was a far better understanding of my own spiritual nature—a strange gift indeed from an emissary of Hades.

Most important in my mind is that I have never been forced, or even asked, to do anything whatsoever. The ideas are simply presented to me and I am perfectly free, as you are, to accept or reject them, to act upon or ignore them as I see fit.

The only strange part of the experience is that I remember what never happened to me in this physical life and write down thoughts that are not my own—though I later adopt most of them after trying them on for size.

Try reading one of Storyteller's tales aloud, then do the same with my comments. It is easy to see that they did not come from the same mind. I only wish I could learn to write with the rhythm and brilliance of phrase which he seems to handle so easily.

I am able to break off a tale in the middle to attend to the chores of my small homestead or greet the infrequent visitor, and often do so. That the tale picks up where it left off may be due to Storyteller's view of time, which I will quote later in this chapter. The idea of possession simply does not hold up.

Next, I examined the idea that I might be an unconscious medium, and Storyteller a spirit guide, although Storyteller seemed as alive as I was.

I am not an expert on mediums, but have some knowledge of the subject. My understanding is that a medium allows his/her physical form to be used by someone who has died so that they may communicate with the world of the living. In the seances I have attended, the medium had to be told afterward what was said and what occurred.

I am perfectly aware of myself **as** myself at all times. During these experiences I enter no trance or supernatural state. I am always perfectly aware of my surroundings with the single exception of the experience told of in the first chapter. I think Storyteller used shock tactics in that instance to gain my attention.

Automatic writing at first seemed a logical explanation, but on closer examination there were important differences.

In automatic writing the mind is focused elsewhere and the hand writes a message on its own, so to speak. Depending on your beliefs, the message comes from the writer's subconscious, or from another personality—either dead or a spirit who never wore flesh. As in the case of the medium, the writer is unaware of the content of the message till he or she reads it.

I, on the other hand, am focused on each word as I write it. I am aware of the content of the tale as I go along. I simply write down the words I remember as though taking dictation. I hear Storyteller speak but it is more like a long-lost memory than words I am hearing for the first time.

At this time, I had discovered many things that Storyteller was **not** but seemed little closer to discovering what he was.

Finally, following the promptings of my inner self, I directed the question inward with all the force and emotion I could muster, then dismissed it from my physical mind. Several days later, when I sat down to write what I expected to be another tale, I received the following:

> I am Storyteller. I am the entity you met at the ancient home of the Nanina and yet I am also much more.
> In one way, I am a larger portion of his soul. In another, I am the collective soul of all the many Storytellers of the Nanina throughout their physical existence as a people. I stand by to guide them and to keep the stories true.
> In physical terms, I come to you across many seasons of time, and yet there is no time to cross because time, as you

perceive it, exists only in the beating of your hearts and in the thoughts of your mind.[1]

The physical portion of Storyteller is and was as amazed as you at your mutual adventure but was better equipped by his beliefs to integrate it into his life than you were.

What has happened is rare but has happened before and will again. A great advantage of this happening over most others is that the information being passed is of much benefit to the hearer and those in his "time."

You have felt the present aliveness of Storyteller. He and all his people exist now in the same space which you inhabit, as do all other dwellers in different "times," and yet your separation is as great as the two ends of the universe.

As your idea of time is a construction of your physical minds, so is space as you understand it; yet the construction is as binding on you in your physical state as if it were encased in the hardest stone.

These were among the laws which you, yourselves, adopted at the beginning of time, and you are now free to break them only when not dwelling in the flesh. Your larger soul, however, is not bound by them and you may transcend them at times by returning your focus to it.

All of this is difficult to explain in terms which you can understand with the physical mind, but we shall do the best we can.

When the Creator made individual souls out of his being, they were not created one at a time but in groups, each group sharing a collective soul in addition to their individual souls. You might think of these individuals as soul mates.

Although any soul may communicate with any other through the Creator, and constantly does so, the communication between soul mates flows more freely. They often communicate directly, one to another. Such is the case between Storyteller's soul and yours. In most cases, the communication remains within the larger soul, and the physical self is unaware of it.

Storyteller—the one with which you are familiar— how-

---

[1] Some scientists theorize that our sense of time is produced by the jumping of the nerve impulses across the synapses (nerve endings) and that we unconsciously measure it by such bodily processes as the beating of our hearts.

ever, is uniquely attuned to his greater self and better able to use this innate knowledge than most physical selves.

In your case, your almost lifelong search, for you knew not what, makes you a better listener than most physical selves.

Perceiving this opportunity and seeing the worthwhile knowledge that could be passed, one to another, I elected to act as bridge and smooth the way for this passage.

Thus the information is clearer and easier for the physical self to hear.

Be aware that much of this information is intended to stir the listener's consciousness so that it may perceive other information contained within its own soul.

We shall give as much information as we can in physical terms, but the more important information will come from the hearer's soul simply as a **knowing** without the intervention of the physical senses.

Some distortion is unavoidable, but we shall correct this where possible.[2] I emphasize that much of the information is reduced to proportions that may be assimilated by the physical brain. It is not that it is untrue but rather that it is not the whole truth, which would be unintelligible to you in your present state.

As much additional truth as the individual hearer can assimilate is to be found within his or her own soul. Turn your gaze inward and behold your soul.

We shall give no exercises or techniques of mind manipulation, for a technique of use to one may be worthless to another. Search out your own if you wish. What is needed is a change in **attitude**. If you question your soul but do not really expect an answer, you will not perceive it when it is forthcoming.

Now I answer a question which you wished to ask but did not.

Storyteller's voice comes to you in a language that you understand, yet it is impossible that he could have known your tongue.

---

[2] After writing down a tale, I normally put it aside for several days, then read it aloud. On occasion I find myself reading one word or phrase aloud, while hearing another version in my head. The tale is corrected to the new version.

Souls do not communicate in words, as you do. They communicate in a way that is difficult, if not impossible, to you in the physical realm. Think of it as mutual **knowing** and you will not be far off the mark.

Your soul and Storyteller's communicate directly, one to the other. Your spiritual mind then translates this **knowing** into language which your physical mind perceives as a voice. The personality of Storyteller is retained through the accent which you hear and the gestures you use when telling his tales.[3]

I have spoken as though there were divisions between the physical mind, spiritual mind, soul, collective soul and Creator. This was done to better get the idea across. There are actually no divisions. All are one and one is all. To look into the eyes of your fellow humans is to see the Creator, though your physical selves have difficulty perceiving this truth. To behold a blade of grass is to meet the Creator face to face.

Remember that your task is to **create**, not necessarily in visible things alone, for an idea is as great a creation as the finest tool or bow. Do so joyfully because each creation—physical, mental or emotional—adds to the being of the Creator and thus to your own, for the Creator is as much a part of you as you are of the Creator. Keep in mind at all times that you are an **essential** part of creation.

I return now to my role as bridge. I shall leave all further telling of tales and teaching of truths to the StoryTeller you know. He is much better at it than I.[4]

As so often happens, this communication answers the questions that I asked but raises ten more for each one it answers. We must not be dismayed by this because any good theoretical scientist knows that the most difficult step is the first one—finding

---

[3] When I read a tale aloud, I begin in my own voice. Within one or two lines I invariably fall into Storyteller's accent and rhythm and find myself using his gestures.

[4] Whereas Storyteller's vocal effects and gestures are so dramatic and compelling that one becomes lost in the tale he is relating, this communication was given in the style of a schoolroom lecture. The material itself is certainly engrossing, but no attempt was made to dramatize it.

the right question to ask. The rest usually falls into place once the proper amount of work is done.

Although we have all of eternity at our disposal, we shall apparently never know all the answers. Like the Creator, we grow forever. The essential nature of the Creator is to create, in this case to create himself through us. Thus as a part of the Creator, we grow with and in his being forever.

The collective consciousness of the story teller informs us that the entire truth of our physical existence would be unintelligible to us, but surely the time will come when we can perceive it. At that time, however, we will have grown into a greater being and shall face new questions that we cannot now imagine.

The statements concerning the true nature of space and time leave us feeling like strangers in a strange land. If all ages of the Earth share the same space with us, this may help to explain my experience in New Mexico. It would not have been necessary for me to literally travel back in time. It would only be necessary for me to, so to speak, change my focus. I remember how, at the time, things began to grow dim and hazy and I could not focus on anything. When my vision cleared, I was focused on the "time" of Storyteller.

At the risk of using logic to try to solve an essentially spiritual puzzle, another intriguing possibility occurs to me. By changing the focus of our inner eye (the eye of the soul), we should be able to influence both past and future as we now influence the present.

Can we then, theoretically at least, go back and change a past action we now regret?

If all time shares our present space, are there past and future selves at our very elbow? Can we, by changing focus, meet ourselves face to face?

At this point my mind balks like an old mule and refuses to carry me any further. I begin to realize why we bound ourselves to certain laws when donning the flesh.

Most of us have held some rather vague notion of the soul as something inactive and more or less unchanging till after death. Now, however, we are told that our soul is something alive and vital, a connection directly to the Creator— that it perceives and participates in everything we do, say, think, and feel. Indeed, the very earth on which we walk is part of it, and through it a part of the Creator. Not something the Creator made, mind you, but **part** of the Creator.

LIVE YOUR SOUL

In the present age, many of us seem to be running in all directions trying to find ourselves.

Our youth go to India to study under a guru or join one of the cults or fringe groups in our own land.

Older people, and those in business, eagerly rush from channeling to crystal therapy to whatever the current innovation is.

Books by the thousands are sold to teach us Yoga, meditation, understanding ourselves— and so ad infinitum.

Don't misunderstand me; I enthusiastically endorse any search for the inner self. I can well testify that even the strangest tree may bear good fruit.

Sooner or later we reach the point where we ask, "Now that I'm getting the hang of this, what do I do with it?"

The Nanina answer, "Live it. Live your soul."

Memories

The vain young woman stands looking at a tangle of briers. Her mouth waters and her belly hungers at sight of the sweet, ripe berries within.

She looks at the smooth young skin of her arms and breasts and says, "I cannot go in there. My skin is beautiful. The thorns would scratch my arms and legs and breasts. The berries would stain my hands and lips, and for days I would be ugly." Sadly, she turns away.

The children plunge into the brier patch like javelina boars. The briers rake and scratch their tender skin in vain as their treasure is stripped from them.

Laughing and shouting, they stuff berries into their mouths with both hands, until their faces and bodies are as blotched as the old rock snake lying in the sun. They hear the birds sing around them and startle rabbits into flight. They feel the warmth of *Babishta Hetchiyu*, Bright Father, the sun, on their heads and backs.

Naked and scratched, they run home laughing, the skirts of the girls and the loincloths of the boys stuffed with berries and carried in their hands.

Proudly they stand as one by one the women of the Nanina come to praise the fineness of the berries and depart with bowls of them to be eaten around the hearth that evening.

The vain young woman takes her share and they are good— but not as good as those eaten by the children in the berry patch.

Long seasons afterward, the woman sits by the fire. No longer young, her skin is now wrinkled, her breasts sagging, the taste of her bowl of berries long forgotten. A man and woman, now mated and with children of their own, sit with her.

The young woman touches the man's hand and asks, "Do you remember the year when the berries were **so** good?"

He smiles, and once again they feel the sun and taste the berries with the tongue of their memory. Their chests are warm with an old pride as they remember the praise of the women as they shared their bounty.

The old woman frowns as she searches her memory, but she can remember—nothing.

I tell you now. Seize the joy of the moment and that moment will feed your soul with its memory for all eternity.

I sometimes remember how I saw with both my own eyes and those of Storyteller, the first and only time I saw him in the flesh.

Does this perhaps mean that he remembers our age through my mind in the same way that I remember the world of the Nanina through his?

Is this why he has chosen these particular tales to tell? It seems to me that they are particularly appropriate to our times. They give us a fresh perspective on our being and a new angle from which to attack modern problems.

Consider this: as a man eats his evening meal, he keeps one eye on the television set. He watches as a soldier in some distant war has his life torn from him in a hail of bullets. "Don't know what the world's coming to," he mutters, washing down the last bit with a cup of coffee. Shortly, the scene is forgotten.

Later that evening his teenage son carelessly backs the car over his new tulip bed. His digestion is ruined. He rants and raves. That night he tosses and turns, unable to sleep in his anger.

Are his reactions to these two incidents out of proportion? Not at all. The difference is that he was a participant in one and not in the other.

The man killed before his eyes on TV was not "real." He was merely a picture on the screen of a box. He did not know him, could do nothing to help him, and the death was already over by the time he viewed it.

The loss of the tulips was something which touched his life directly. With loving care he had dug the bed, adding precisely the right amount and kind of fertilizer. He had positioned the bulbs just so to get a certain effect. In his mind's eye he had already seen them in bloom and eagerly awaited the day when he could view them in all their glory. It is quite natural that he should be more upset over the "lesser" incident. It affected his life far more than the death of the anonymous soldier.

Most of us have spent countless hours in front of our TV set. How many times have you seen something that is likely to be fondly recalled twenty years later? That same amount of time spent any number of other ways may well produce such a memory.

Your soul even now views this reality through your eyes. Will you show it reruns of soap operas or sunsets? The choice is entirely in your hands.

Go outside and look at a flower. No—I mean **look** at a flower. See the delicate differences of shading within it. Watch how the sun plays across it as it shifts in the wind. Feel the flow of the life force within it. Make of the flower an emotional experience. Any three-year-old can teach you. Children remember how.

Stop being a spectator. Participate in life. Secondhand emotions are poor fare indeed to nourish a soul.

Charge into your experiences and strip them of their fruit. To hell with the thorns. Share your bounty of joy with all about you. In a word, **live**!

Stress

The toolmaker selects a flint stone carefully. He examines it and it seems suitable. He strikes it sharply with the hammer stone, but the flint perceives only that it is being struck. It struggles against the toolmaker and so shatters and is cast aside.

He selects another, and this flint does not perceive the striking as an attack. It can feel that it is being shaped. It does not struggle. The shard splits off cleanly and after final shaping with a spur from a deer's antler, it is a fine scraper.

The arrow maker chooses sections of birch logs. Inserting a hardwood wedge into a crack caused by drying, he taps it with a mallet.

Some wood resists and in the struggle the wood twists and splinters. He tosses them toward the fire to be burned by the women as they cook.

Others split cleanly in response to his efforts. These logs perceive that they are becoming something greater than they had been.

The arrow maker takes the stone scraper and scrapes the wood perfectly straight and smooth.

The cooperation of the stone, which is now a scraper, and the logs, which are becoming arrow shafts, will produce fine arrows which will be prized and cared for by the Nanina hunters.

So do you sometimes perceive yourselves as scraped and struck by misfortune and illness, but it may be that your soul is shaping you into something greater than you had been.

Unlike the tool and arrow makers, your soul will never cast you aside for you are precious—a very part of the being of the Creator. If you struggle against your soul's intentions however, you will never be what you could have been had you perceived its intentions and allowed yourself to be shaped more easily.

I tell you now. Live your soul. Help it in its efforts to shape your being. Be a fine arrow in the Creator's bundle. He will prize and care for you even after the end of time.

First allow me to remind you that your soul is not some outside force inflicting these misfortunes on you. It **is** you, and in a deeper part of your being you well know what is happening and why.

The ill fortunes of the flint and logs in this tale were not caused by the striking of the toolmaker or the splitting of the arrow maker, but by their struggles against them.

A better rapport with your own soul will result in more complete understanding of the shaping process and a fuller participation in it.

Less stress will thus be produced, and it is this stress which appears in the physical realm as misfortune and illness.

It is revealing of the Nanina way that they had no word for evil. The very idea was foreign to their way of thinking. When misfortune or illness struck, the Nanina would often say, "What is— is. It is all part of the Creator."

The nearest the Nanina approached to the idea of evil was their concept of *korak. Korak* was a state of disharmony with those around you, by implication a disharmony with one's own soul.

A person in a state of *korak* was looked upon as someone in need of being gently guided back into harmony. Certainly they were not shunned as we shun "evil" people.

One wonders how many of those "evil" men and women we keep behind bars would be living full lives today had our society adopted this idea, gently guiding them back into harmony in their youth.

The Nanina also had no words for murder, robbery or rape, nor did they need any.

Opportunity

The men had been working for many days. With stone axes, chisels and wedges, they were cutting oak trees. They wished to split the wood into thin strips for making baskets much sturdier and longer-lasting than willow baskets.

One of the men struck with his axe and it sank deeply, far too deeply. When the man pulled the axe free, black foul-smelling water gushed out. The tree was rotted inside.

In disgust the men turned away. The tree was useless to them.

The tanner, however, had been working alongside the men in hope of this very thing. He rushed over with the water skins he had brought and caught the liquid. To him it was precious for it would tan fine skins much tougher and of a richer color than skins tanned with ashes and smoke.

An old man knew where the wild bees lived. He listened to the sound of the hive and thought that the bees would soon swarm. He wished the new swarm to come and live close to his hut. He would protect them from harm and the bees would give him fine, sweet honey. He had spoken to the soul of the bees and they were willing to do this, but he had nothing to offer them for a home.

When the tanner told him of the tree, he went there with some friends and finished cutting it down. The hollow trunk would make several fine beehives.

Plant-Talking Woman (a healer of the Nanina, see next chapter) went to where the treetop lay. She gathered the unripe acorns and the galls which wasps make on the leaves of hollow oaks. From them, she made a healing salve for cuts, scrapes and burns.

Rabbits and quail found the treetop a fine place to nest and shelter from hawks.

The men who had been cutting the tree went home and for a long time after spoke sadly of the hard work they had done only to find the tree useless.

As they sat and spoke of their bad fortune, they wore new knee-length moccasins soled with leather tanned by the fluid in the tree.

They ate toasted grain mixed with honey given by the bees who lived in the hollow trunk.

The scrapes on the knees of their children, the burns of the women at the cooking fires and their own hurts were soothed by Plant-Talking Woman's salve.

They cooked fat rabbits and ate quail eggs from the animals sheltering in the treetop.

I tell you now. What you perceive as misfortune is often a gift of your soul, but you must learn to look deeply if you would understand this.

How often in this existence do we see ourselves as failures in one enterprise or another! Our larger self often has a truer picture of the goal than we do.

The men in this tale saw themselves as thwarted in their attempt; but was the true goal the making of baskets? The larger goal was surely to make life easier for themselves and for all the Nanina.

This goal was reached many times over. Instead of the single benefit of the baskets, life was made easier in numerous ways, most of them lasting far longer than the baskets would have.

Sir Alexander Fleming was breeding a germ culture. When the culture began dying, he could have simply dumped it and started over, as most would have. Instead he took that extra step. He investigated to find out **why** it was failing. Penicillin was the outcome of that question, and countless lives are saved every year because he took that step.

How many before him had almost made the same discovery, only to let it slip through their hands because they accepted the "failure"!

Any apparent failure may have within it the seeds of a larger success. If we do not plant and nurture those seeds, they will never grow.

Exchanges

The child walks to the cooking fire. Toasted grain and roasted fish lie on the serving stone. The child takes a piece of roasted fish and chews a mouthful of toasted grain, then turns to leave.

The woman watches. She calls out to the child, but she does not ask, "Whose child are you?" or "What will your mother give me in exchange for the fish and grain?"

The child is a child and so is welcome at any hut and free to sleep in any bed when tired. It is a child of all the Nanina.

The woman has pounded some starch from the roots of water plants. She has boiled it with grain, nuts and honey to make a pudding and only wishes the child to have some.

Her eyes are tender and her heart warm as she watches the child eat.

The child has received food and the woman feels love. It is a fine exchange.

The hunter returns from a narrow wood along a stream. His luck and skill have been good today. He has three rabbits, five ducks, and his net has caught two fat geese.

Looking neither right nor left, he strides to the center of the hut group and squats, the game in a pile before him.

One by one the women come from the huts and take what they need, praising the fine quality of the game as they do so.

The Nanina will eat fine stew tonight, and the hunter's chest is large with pride. It is a fine exchange.

The hunter's leggings have been torn by brush along the stream. A man has tanned some hides, and his woman has used them to make several pairs of leggings.

She does not shame the hunter by waiting till he asks for them. She walks to the hunter's hut and lays them on his bed. She asks no thanks, for then the gift would not be from the heart and soul.

The hunter has new leggings to protect him from thorns. The woman is proud that the Nanina will see and admire her work wherever the hunter goes. It is a fine exchange.

As the food was freely given to the child, the game shared with any who needed it, and the leggings given to the hunter, so does your soul accept what is given by the Creator and freely offer it to you.

I tell you now. Take what is given and use it joyfully. Your soul and the Creator will share this joy with you, and all will grow in their being. It is a fine exchange.

This is a "made up on the spot" tale which was told for the first time not to the Nanina, but to us. The gentle rebuke for the greedy ways of our present society convinces me that Storyteller is indeed aware of us and our modern way of life.

Your soul and the Creator ask only that you use and enjoy what is given. Your constant praise is not required, only your joy. The gifts belong to you by right, as a part of creation, just as the food belonged to the child because it was a child.

The Creator grows in our joy and pride and by watching the growth in our being. As Storyteller says, "It is a fine exchange."

This tale gives some insight into the Nanina way of life. The next chapter tells what I remember of that way.

5

THE NANINA CULTURE
—Plant-Talking Woman

Who were the Nanina? Where did they come from? I can only
speculate. I remember much of Nanina history during Storyteller's
life and a fair amount of what came after, but know nothing of what
came before. Why this should be, I have no idea. I would have
expected it to be the other way around.

Many Indians of the Americas, both North and South, have
legends of a light-skinned people who lived here many years ago.
These people were renowned as spiritual teachers. For some
unknown reason they left, but were expected to return one day.

The Aztecs mistakenly identified Cortez and his small army as
the returning teachers, and this is one factor in their quick defeat.
Alas, these bloodthirsty pirates bore no resemblance to the teachers other than their light skin.

No less than Thor Heyerdahl gave some credence to these tales,
and the voyage of the *Kon Tiki* was to prove that they could have
reached the islands of the South Pacific.

Perhaps the Nanina were a remnant of these people, somehow
left behind when the rest departed.

If this is so, the separation must have taken place a very long
time ago for Storyteller lived about three thousand years ago and

his people had already forgotten their origins. It may be significant that although they lived far inland, they did have knowledge of the seas, as we have seen in Storyteller's tale of Creation.

The Nanina had no contact with other people, with one notable exception. So isolated were they that they had forgotten that the rest of the world was inhabited.

The single exception was Plant-Talking Woman who appeared early one morning, simply walking over a hill and into their settlement. As her skin was darker than the Nanina, she was probably Indian. Since she played such a large part in Storyteller's life, I will give a brief history of her stay with the Nanina.

Though she quickly learned their language, Plant-Talking Woman never revealed where she came from or why she came. Her very name was bestowed on her by the Nanina, who never learned her original name.[1]

She quickly gained the love and respect of the people, for she was a gifted healer and freely taught any who wished to learn.

Though she was friendly, they could sense a difference in her and she became almost a mystical figure to them.

Mated to Storyteller, she used her knowledge of herbal medicine to avoid having children, explaining to him that the Nanina depended on her and she must be free at all times to tend the sick and injured.

When she had been with the Nanina for seven years, she told Storyteller, to his great joy, that she would bear his child. She lay with him that night and in the morning was gone as mysteriously as she came.

Storyteller easily found her trail, for she made no effort to hide it. He followed her into the high juniper hills for eight days but was never able to bring her into sight.

At the foot of a steep mountain with a flattened top, her trail was marked with a row of stones across it. Storyteller recognized the sign and knew that it meant, "Follow no farther."

On the center stone were a red and a white flower of a type he

---

[1] The name Plant-Talking Woman signified her skill at bringing herself into harmony with the collective consciousness of the various plants. She was thus able to discern the medicinal properties of any plant, whether familiar with it or not.

had never seen before and a tiny pouch of seeds. Sadly, Storyteller returned to his people, taking the flowers and seeds with him.

He scattered the minute seeds over the hills, and in a few years the flowers were sprinkled all across them.

The Nanina discovered that the flowers were a powerful medicinal herb which aided other herbs in the curing of diseases. Until the Nanina ceased to exist as a people, the flowers were called "Plant-Talking Woman's Last Gift." Storyteller was never mated to another woman.[2]

---

[2] I know and have a special rapport with the one who stands in the same relation to Plant-Talking Woman that I have to Storyteller. Alas, she and her soul mate are unaware of one another in their physical minds, though communicating frequently in their spiritual minds.

The climate of the part of New Mexico inhabited by the Nanina was more temperate and moist then. Summer was mild in that region and the winter both warmer and of shorter duration than now.

The area was so well drained that it never flooded and the rain so dependable that drought was rare. Streams, ponds and lakes held a never-ending supply of fish, crayfish and fresh-water clams. Wild ducks and geese visited them during their migrations and often wintered there.

The narrow woods along the streams held an abundance of small game, and two days' walk north the wooded hills with their deer could be found. To my surprise, I found no memory of buffalo.

Since life was easy, the people had an abundance of free time and used it wisely in studying and discussing their own spiritual nature.

There was no formal religion or priesthood. Each man or woman was their own shaman and there was no "right" or "wrong" view of spiritual matters. Religion was a matter between each person and their own soul and evolved constantly as comprehension grew.

Each sex tended to the tasks that seemed "natural." This usually meant that men brought in the meat and tended to tasks away from home while women gathered grain, cooked and tended to household tasks. But it was not unusual to find a woman hunting when she had no nursing children, or a man tending the hearth if so inclined.

It would never occur to a Nanina that one sex or any one person was superior to another except on a superficial level.

No one was ever appointed or elected as leader. A leader was simply one whom the others followed of their own free will and they were free to accept or ignore the leader's advice. No Nanina would ever try to give orders to another.

We hear the morals in Storyteller's tales for the first time, but the Nanina were well aware of these truths; and the tales were meant to serve as reminders, for Storyteller knew how easy it is to forget spiritual matters in the distraction of physical existence.

Perhaps the key to the Nanina way was the fact that no person was made to feel like an outsider. Each was part of the greater society and accepted as such. No Nanina ever did anything without considering its effect on others.

As you may have observed in the tales, nothing was done

selfishly. People finding berries brought enough for those in their hut group. A man tanning leather would gather the hides of his neighbors and tan them also. A woman making a skirt or loincloth would make several extra. The surplus was given freely to any who needed it. Nothing was ever sold, bartered or hoarded, thus no one was richer or poorer in material goods than any others.

They were not innocent of the concept of personal property. A person's bow, throwing stick, clothing, clay cooking pots (but not water pots), and some other items of personal use were considered to belong to someone, and custom dictated that they never be touched by the hand of another unless that person indicated their permission, for instance by handing a pot of food to another. Children too young to understand were not bound by this custom until they grew old enough to adopt it on their own.

The idea of theft in such a society becomes ridiculous. A person seeing a need in another filled that need as a matter of course. The one in need was not required to ask for it, or even thank the giver. It was simply the natural thing to do. The pride of the giver and the shared joy of the receiver were all the payment required.

A man and woman deciding to become mated first went to the Storyteller. He carried the genealogy of the tribe in his head and could trace the relationship of any two people. If they were not too closely related, they announced their mating at ten hearths. At each hearth they received a token gift expressing the approval of that household. Such gifts of congratulation might include a handful of grain, a bone needle, a stone knife or whatever else the giver might have which would be handy in setting up a household. The couple were then considered as husband and wife. Separation could be accomplished in the same simple way, this time giving rather than receiving gifts. This was very rare.

Children were not considered as "belonging" to someone, as they unfortunately are in our society. They were simply the children of the Nanina. The mother had primary care of a child till it was old enough to walk, though a crying child was commonly picked up and nursed by the nearest woman who had milk.

After the child was old enough to walk well, it was free to go wherever it wished. All adults habitually kept an eye on any child in sight to keep it from harm.

The child knew who its parents were and had a special relationship with them, but could help itself to food at any hearth, sleep in any hut, or seek comfort from any adult when it had an upset stomach or skinned its knee.

Children were gently guided in their growth. They were seldom scolded, and the Nanina would be shocked at our practice of striking children and absolutely horrified at the guilt which our society constantly heaps upon them.

The result of this relaxed form of child-rearing was an adult with a firm sense of self-worth and a society that could not even conceive of striking another, of murder or assault, let alone war.

The Nanina had a distinctive manner of speech. I think of it as verbal shorthand. Storyteller's tales are far more detailed in English than they would be in his native language.

The Nanina were a small tribe, at their height numbering only about three hundred, and so were, as the modern idiom has it, "into each other's heads." Only a few key words were usually required to get an idea across.

Suppose, for instance, a group of us was working at some distance from home. One of us might say something such as "We'd better put up our tools and go home. It'll be dark soon." A Nanina would simply look at the sky and say "*Hiyasu kori*" meaning "night" and expect his fellows to come to the appropriate conclusions on their own.

Here is a Nanina lullaby which will illustrate what I mean.[3] I will give it first in the Nanina tongue. then in a literal word-for-word translation, and finally in English (free translation).

NANINA LULLABY
Kora shay
Whishtan horay
Nan chyan parayi
Horeste
Horeste, hiyasu kori
Nan chyan parayi
Hwashtay

---

3 This lullaby is the only song I remember. It was also the first of my Nanina memories. One night as I prepared to sleep I found myself humming a tune I didn't place. Several nights later, the Nanina words came into my mind, slowly and painfully compared to the easy flow I now enjoy. I think perhaps it was a training exercise, for soon afterward Storyteller's first tale began.

Literal Translation
Floating
Cloud apart
Child dream
Departing
Leaving night
Child soul
Examine

As you can see, this is almost gibberish to us, yet it makes perfect sense once you learn to fill in between the lines, as a Nanina would without a second thought. The result would be subtly different for each hearer but would be somewhere near the following free translation.

Float away
On your separate cloud
The dream child
Takes you away
Upon your nightly journeying
The depths of your soul
To survey

This manner of speech served their mental framework very well. Much in the manner of Japanese haiku poetry, it simply supplied the skeleton which the hearer fleshed out as his or her individual personality dictated. They used a more detailed form of speech to explain a concept or spiritual insight with which the hearer was unlikely to be familiar.

You may well be thinking that it was far easier for the Nanina, whose physical needs were so easily satisfied, to devote their time to spiritual matters than it is for you to do so.

Remember what has been pointed out. Our everyday environment is our soul's expression in the physical world. Bringing that expression into focus is our task. The pollution, wars, poverty and hunger we see about us may well be a reflection of our collective disharmony with our greater selves. This disharmony brings about an imperfect rendition of the inner knowledge which our soul constantly sends to us.

We have been trying for a long time to solve our problems

through physical means, only to see each solution bring problems worse than the ones it solves.

The problem of mobility is solved by motor vehicles which slaughter countless innocents each year and threaten to strangle us in their fumes.

The problem of hunger is solved by farming methods which destroy our precious topsoil, producing so much food in some nations that farmers must be bribed to stop producing while people in neighboring nations starve before our eyes.

The problem of crime is solved by passing stricter laws which place so many behind bars that new prisons are overcrowded before the paint is dry. The police are seen as enemies by the very taxpayers who hire them. Laws become so complicated that the advice of a lawyer is necessary for the simplest act. Judges cannot agree on what the laws say.

The problem of war is solved by inventing weapons so terrible that none dare use them. With so many fingers poised on so many doomsday buttons, we live in terror lest one of them twitch.

I am not so naive as to think that we can adopt the Nanina way in its entirety. Ours is a different world with different problems. They have shown us a way to solve these problems, however, by looking inward rather than outward for solutions. When we are in harmony with our greater self, problems have a way of evaporating.

My own homestead is forty acres of ridge land that no one ever bothered with. Anyone can see that the land is poorly suited to farming or homesteading, yet with only a few hours of work, done at a leisurely pace, virtually all my needs are met. All accounts of a self-sufficient lifestyle emphasize the many hours of hard work necessary, yet that has not been my experience.

I have only begun to comprehend what Storyteller has to teach, yet my life is now so much more satisfying that I look back in dismay at my former lifestyle.

Perhaps someday my forty acres of Goat's Bluff can become the nucleus of a small group which will learn to live a saner lifestyle than those around us. A beginning must certainly be made somewhere if there is to be any hope for our society.

6

DREAM YOUR SOUL

The Nanina considered the dream state and the work done there every bit as important as the waking state.

In the dream state, our soul communicates openly with the physical self, teaching lessons and concepts that cannot be expressed in words. Undistracted by the world of flesh and matter, the physical self is more receptive to such communication in this state.

Symbols are the language of the dream world. These symbols must be contemplated calmly and the contents felt rather than understood through logic and intellect.

In our insistence on logic, valuable information is lost to us. We stand by feeling helpless as our reality decays into turmoil.

Here is a tale used by Storyteller to point out the proper use of dreams.

Symbols

A wise hunter wishes to become more successful at taking deer. He goes to a remote pond where he will not be disturbed. Squatting, he begins sketching in the sand with a sharp stick.

Slowly and carefully, he scratches pictures of deer into the sand, making each more detailed than the last.[1] As he does so, he calls to mind what he has observed of deer and their ways.

In drawing the muzzles, he remembers the deer browsing and observes in this memory the different brush they eat at different seasons. He watches in his mind as they water and tries to feel why they water here and not there.

As he draws the head, he watches its motion in his mind as it turns this way and that, seeing and scenting its environment.

He draws the eye, feeling why it notices one thing and not another.

In drawing the ear, he watches it twist and turn, always listening.

Drawing the legs, he sees them run and leap over obstacles, trying to feel why the deer chooses a particular path of flight, and what pattern that flight will take.

After several days of this remembering and observing, he sits for a long time in contemplation of the collective soul of deer, bringing himself into harmony with it and feeling his soul's relationship with that of deer.

When next he goes to the wooded hills, he will be able to think as a deer and anticipate its actions. His soul will be in harmony with the animals and he will be able to take it with the proper respect and reverence for it and its part in the being of the Creator.

The life force of the deer will flow smoothly into the life force of the Nanina, becoming part of them and nourishing their bodies and souls.[2]

---

[1] Could this be an explanation for rock and cave paintings left by ancient cultures throughout the world?

[2] Compare this with the attitude of the modern hunter who is likely to mount the head as a trophy to brag about while the rest is discarded as mere garbage. Proper respect for the animal requires the fullest possible use of it, both in the physical and spiritual sense.

Perhaps this lack of harmony with the spirit of our animals explains why the meat pouring forth from our slaughterhouses is increasingly found to be unhealthy for us.

So does your soul draw pictures in the sand of your dreams. As the pictures which the hunter drew were not the deer but symbols which served to focus and bring into harmony his soul and that of deer, thus are the pictures drawn by your soul meant to serve as symbols and bring into harmony your physical and spiritual being.

I tell you now. Watch carefully as your soul draws its pictures. **Remember** what you observe. Allow your mind and soul to flow freely into one another. Both your physical and spiritual being will be nourished and grow.

The language of your greater self during the dream state is not in words but in symbols. The interpretation of those symbols is your task and it is seldom of any use to turn to another for help.

Some will tell you that certain dream symbols are universal. Flying, for instance, is said to be an expression of freedom. If, however, you have survived an aircraft accident, flying to you may represent great danger. Your inner self will use flying in this context when communicating with you. You must ask yourself what the symbol means to you in emotional terms.

Dream books will give long lists of symbols, assigning definite meanings to each, seemingly with great authority. They are not only useless, but can be downright misleading.

It often seems to us that our dreams are jumbled nonsense. A stone becomes a frog which jumps into a puddle which is really a field of flowers.

Let's examine this as an example. First, feel what each symbol means to you. Is a stone cold and unfeeling or a sun-warmed part of *Hiyei Hiyasu*? Is a frog a comical clown or a slimy repulsive creature? Go through each symbol, feeling the emotional content, and note how one changes into another. You should then be able to interpret it, not by logic, but by intuition. You will **know** when you are right.

Remember that in the dream state we are temporarily out of the flesh. Physical laws no longer bind us. Time does not flow in the straight line we are accustomed to.

In our physical existence we take some action to form energy into matter or mold our environment, and there is a time lag, sometimes of considerable duration, before we see the result. In the dream state we see that result immediately. We play with energy as a child does with clay, molding one thing, then another, and yet another, all with the same raw material, molding stones, frogs, puddles and flowers, using the raw energy flowing from the Creator.

Logic has little or no meaning here. Our higher self participates in mutual **knowing** with other beings, and what our physical mind retains on waking is only that part which we have been able to capture as symbols. Though seemingly fragmentary, these symbols contain whatever parts of this communication are pertinent to our present physical state.

More active participation by the physical self in our dreams will broaden this useful knowledge, and we can then apply it in our everyday lives.

Once we learn to become participants in, rather than merely observers of, our dreams, we are able to try out changes in our environment or solutions to our problems, observing the results immediately, molding and remolding till we find the result which seems best to us.

Remember that this activity is all done symbolically and must be interpreted as a **knowing** rather than reasoned out by logic.

For Storyteller's views on another type of dreaming, read this next tale.

Quarry

A group of children listened as an old woman reminisced about how she once caught crayfish. She spoke of how she would boil and peel the tails, then dip them in a sauce made of the oil of hickory nuts mixed with wild garlic. She told of her pleasure as she shared them with neighboring hearths. They enjoyed hearing the old woman speak.

A girl imagined her pride if she could catch some crayfish and give them to the old woman. She asked a boy to go with her, but he said the net was torn and ran off to play. The girl got some bark twine from her father and mended the net. She asked another boy, but he said the trap was broken and went to sit by the fire. A woman weaving baskets gave the girl some willow splits and showed her how to patch the trap. The next boy said they had no bait for the trap, and the one after that said that the winter had been too cold and the crayfish would be thin with watery meat in their tails.

The girl put the net and trap into a basket and went to the pond. A man was fishing there and he gave her the heads of several fish and showed her how to bait and set the trap.

The crayfish were fine and fat. Many came to the trap to eat the fish. Each scoop of the net caught several more.

By the end of the day the girl had filled the basket with netted crayfish and the trap held many more.

Her chest was large with pride as she heard the old woman laughing in joy, and she shared her pleasure at once again having a bounty to share with others.

The being of the girl grew that day. At the sunset the boys were no more than they had been at the sunrise.

So does your soul tell you in your dreams many tales of what might be. You can always find good reasons for not bringing these tales about, but unless you do so, where will your joy arise, and how will you grow in your being?

I tell you now. Mend the nets, patch the traps and catch the dreams that are shown to you. The chest of your soul will grow large in its pride and you will grow in your being.

The Nanina considered daydreaming akin to sleep dreaming but more physically oriented. The dreams which arise during daydreaming are easier to translate into everyday activity. They do not have the spiritual content of sleep dreaming, but are more pertinent to physical reality.

In our society, children are constantly berated for "mooning about" and admonished to go out and play. The Nanina would never disturb someone who is obviously daydreaming and encouraged it in the children.

It is interesting in this regard that Albert Einstein was put out of school as unteachable because of constant daydreaming. Alexander Graham Bell, Thomas Edison, Henry Ford and many other inventors and innovators of note were great daydreamers. Thomas Edison even took several catnaps each day. People would shake their heads and wonder why they wasted their time dreaming instead of working, never realizing that was what they **were** doing.

I remind you again that we are the soul's focus in physical reality. Energy flows into us from our greater being and is shaped by that focus. Picture yourself as successful in some endeavor and believe in that dream and you are well on your way. The dream provides the focus to bring it into your reality.

This is not to say that working to bring it about is unnecessary, but the work is well begun when you know exactly what it is you are striving for because you have already seen it in your daydreams.

Storyteller comments on this matter in his next tale.

Observation

A hunter is showing a young boy how to move quietly in the woods. He teaches him how to observe the ground as he moves and still know what is going on around him. He shows the boy how to feel what is underfoot before stepping down.

The boy does not see what the man teaches because his mind is busy with thoughts of the game he will bear proudly into many Nanina hut groups.

When the boy goes out to hunt, he snaps dry sticks underfoot. If he looks about for game, his feet tangle in vines and he falls noisily. When he watches the ground, the game slips quietly off and he does not see it. He sees little of what is happening around him and understands little of what he does see. He takes no game that day and returns home exhausted.

A woman is teaching a young girl how to make fine grass

baskets. She teaches her the technique of weaving so tightly that the basket will hold even water. She shows her how to work in different colored grasses to form a pattern which will please the eye and heart.

The girl's mind is on the boy who attracts her and she hears little of what the woman says and sees even less of how she weaves.

When she tries to make a basket to show to the boy, the grasses become a tangled mess and the pattern a blotch. She becomes troubled in her spirit and throws the whole thing into the fire. She has nothing to catch the boy's eye and flees into the hut weeping.

So does your soul patiently teach you in your dreams, but your waking mind is distracted by everyday life and you pay little attention. It all becomes a jumble in your mind till you can make no sense of it. The flow of your life loses its smoothness and your spirit is troubled. You exhaust yourself and accomplish nothing.

I tell you now. Calm your mind and carefully observe what you see in your dreams. Become tranquil and **know**. Dream your soul.

This story is an excellent example of how Storyteller often teaches on several levels at one time.

On the one hand we are told the importance of observing and **knowing** our dreams, while on the other we are admonished that we must then apply this **knowing** in our everyday lives.

Both the boy and girl in this tale were daydreaming of worthwhile goals they wished to accomplish but were unwilling to learn and work for those goals.

WIthout the dreaming, we scatter our efforts, not really knowing just what our goals are; and without applying the knowledge we gain, we cannot bring them into our reality. A balance of both is required.

Know this. A dream is just as real a construction as a bridge or house. It remains real in the spiritual realm whether or not we actualize it physically. Indeed, some of our dreams are meant to help us realize the nature of our greater being and are not intended to be brought forth in everyday life.

Realize that the real goal is not to gather the greatest number of physical treasures, as modern man seems to think, but to create and to grow, so that our being constantly enlarges.

Because our society has not realized their importance, use of our dreams is something we must teach ourselves. The first step is to realize that they **are** significant.

Try to remember your dreams when you awaken. Write them down if you wish. Spend a short time feeling their emotional content before arising. When dropping off to sleep, form the intent to remember them in the morning. Soon enough, the recall will become second nature.

The **knowing** will come of its own accord when you learn to accept it. Learn to know what you know and don't concern yourself with how you know. To some this will come easier than to others, but sooner or later it will come if you persist.

Suddenly one night you will realize that you are dreaming. You can now become a participant rather than merely a spectator. You will find that you can be as creative there as you are in waking life.

Be playful in this activity. Life in all its aspects is meant to be joyful, whether in or out of the flesh.

7

CREATION AND
YOUR PART IN IT

As physical selves we live in a particular reality. Though its nature is primarily spiritual, it has its expression in physical terms, in flesh and matter. Its material dimensions are the limited aspects of space and time in which our souls framed it.

Physical reality, as with all existence, is part of the Creator's being. It arose through the endless expansion of the Creator.

Put into terms understandable to the physical mind, the boundaries of spiritual space must continually grow so that the Creator's being may expand into them. The Creator forms groups of souls whose task it is to expand these boundaries. The primary aspects of these souls are individuality and self-awareness, but they forever remain a part of the Creator's being. Each soul has its own identity within the larger soul of the group.

One of the attributes of all souls, individual as well as collective, is free will. This attribute was not specifically bestowed upon us but is a very part of our self-awareness.

Free will is ours by right, not as a gift of a generous God. Without free will there is no individuality, and thus no point to our creation. It follows that neither reward nor punishment is attached to the exercise of this attribute.

For the Creator to say, in effect, "I grant you complete free will but I forbid you to use it except in accordance with my wishes or you shall be punished" is to grant us free will with one hand and snatch it away with the other.

This is not to say that we are free to use our freedom to tyrannize others. Such an act would generate a state of *korak*, disharmony with our inner being, which would inevitably disrupt our personal environment in an unpleasant way. This is not punishment any more than a headache is punishment for being struck on the head. Disharmony merely carries unpleasant consequences within itself.

A group of collective souls began to gather around an idea it was forming as a first step in spiritual expansion. I will term this group a cluster. The souls within this cluster included all of the souls, both individual and collective, who would ever participate in this reality.

The idea took shape through the participation and interaction of all souls in the cluster, which developed its own group consciousness. Our cluster consciousness evolved its idea into the reality which we inhabit, and its physical expression.

Our physical self was still contained within its larger soul at this point. There was no reason to be physically focused on a reality which was not yet physical itself.

Energy forever flows from the Creator in unlimited supply. This energy is undifferentiated—pure energy without form or expression. This is the raw material from which all existence is created.

As the idea took shape, forming the laws which would govern the freedoms and limitations of this reality, the energy began to coalesce into matter, conforming to the idea of our cluster consciousness.

All the matter which forms our physical reality has awareness of itself. Mirroring its spiritual counterpart, it formed an earth consciousness; thus the earth on which we walk is alive and aware.

The Earth's own nature, inherited from the Creator, was to grow and create. It did this through the life-forms which began to appear, providing the earth consciousness with perception of her physical being.

Our souls are constantly aware of this reality in all its spiritual aspects, but since its expression is physical, physical perception must be provided.

Under the guidance of our cluster consciousness, life-forms suitable for this perception were provided by the Earth and became the vehicles inhabited by our souls. We as physical selves were thus individualized. For the first time mankind walked the face of the Earth.

We thus have a dual nature. Our life-forms are the bodies created, nurtured and sustained by *Hiyei Hiyasu*, Mother of All, the Earth. The spiritual selves who inhabit these bodies are portions of our larger souls and provide the senses needed to perceive physical reality. Our personal task is to blend this duality into a harmonious existence, thereby providing the focus of this perception.

Since we are endowed with free will, the choice of this focus is in our hands. The only limitations are the laws by which this reality functions. These laws were freely adopted by us when donning the flesh. They serve as framework to define the idea which our cluster consciousness is developing.

We constantly maintain a balance both delicate and complex and do it so well that we are consciously unaware of it most of the time. Were we not here to provide perception for our souls, this reality would tumble in chaos.

For the most part our focus is on the purely physical aspects of our existence. We seldom allow the spiritual aspects of our reality to enter the physical mind.

The world of flesh and matter is wondrous indeed, but we must become aware that it is an expression of a larger spiritual reality. We have the ability to look in both directions but seem to have forgotten how in our society. When we look only outward, never inward, we lose the balance which keeps us in harmony with our larger soul. This loss of harmony reflects itself in deterioration of our personal environment.

The energy which maintains our reality flows from the Creator in unlimited supply but is undifferentiated. This is tapped by our cluster consciousness and molded into the laws which are its foundation. The energy, now differentiated, is formed by our collective soul into the framework which contains it. Our larger soul takes this, and upon it constructs the spiritual aspects of our reality, depending on us to express those aspects in physical form.

When we consistently ignore our inner sight, we place ourselves in the position of a landscape painter who has never set eyes on the countryside to be portrayed. No matter how well the work is done, it cannot be in harmony with what it is trying to express.

Our souls can perceive physical reality only through us. Our larger self can express itself only where we focus. We may sincerely hope for peace and harmony in the world, but if our attention is on war and strife, that is where the energy enters.

How can it be that our souls were made of the Creator's being and yet always were and always will be? Our physical selves seem to perceive that everything has beginning and end. It appears to us that time flows in a straight line. These are some of the laws which form our reality. We experience this second law as past, present and future. The first law arises from the action of the second. This arrangement of time exists only in our reality, yet exerts so much power over it that we have difficulty imagining any other possibility.

Time, **as we perceive it**, came into being with the creation of our idea in the cluster consciousness and is a construction existing only in our minds. Consider this tale.

Meadow

A woman lives beside a large meadow. On the other side lives an old friend. She remembers the laughter and joy they shared as children and decides to visit her.

It is very far across the meadow and she knows that she can waste no time if she is to spend much time with her friend. She can see the smoke from the hearths across the way and she walks toward this smoke. Her journey is thus kept to a straight line.

She crosses a high spot in the meadow and sees that the soil here is hard red clay. She thinks that it will bake into fine water pots.

At the center of the meadow she passes a spring and sees fine herbs growing near it. She tells herself to remember this spot so that she can gather some on her way back.

On the far side she sees a group of hickory trees and stops

long enough to fill her gathering basket with nuts to share with her friend and those of her hut group.[1]

She has a fine visit, and when her friend asks about the meadow, she tells of the things she has seen. She is proud of her new knowledge and feels that she knows a great deal about the meadow.

A child also lives near the meadow and often goes there. She has no special place to go, she simply goes there to play. She has no need to keep to a straight line.

The child wanders freely in all directions, going forward and back, this way and that, crossing and recrossing her own path.

The child knows of the high spot in the meadow and the red clay there but also knows of another place where there is the black, crumbly dirt so prized by Nanina potters because it bakes blue when applied to pottery. This the woman did not see.

The child knows of the spring and the  herbs but also knows of the pool further down the small stream which flows from it. There are many fine arrowroot plants in the pond prized for the fine starch in their roots. The woman's straight path did not take her to the pool and she knows nothing of it.

The child has gathered the hickory nuts and knows that

1 Nanina women habitually carried a gathering basket whenever leaving the hearth. In a society that sustains itself by gathering, this would, of course, become second nature.

hidden behind the trees is a fine dewberry patch. The woman did not pass that way.

The child knows more of the meadow than the woman because it has no particular direction in which it must go.

So does your straight path through the meadow of time restrict your knowledge of it, even as you take pride in what you have learned there. You know only where you have been— the past; where you are now—the present; and where you are going—the future.

Your soul, like the child, knows much about time which you do not perceive in your straight path.

I tell you now. If you would truly understand the meadow of time, go there with your soul. It can show you many wonders.

As physical selves we are subject to the laws of reality while in the flesh. We can, however, sometimes remove our focus from the flesh and return to our souls for enlightenment. We cannot permanently abandon the concept of past-present-future, nor is it desirable that we do so.

The more we perceive the meaning behind the mask of physical reality, the more efficient we can be as a point of focus for our soul.

To know the true nature of time we must transcend logic and experience it as a **knowing**. The world of logic is in the physical realm and it cannot accompany us on our journey into our deeper being.

I am not telling you to be illogical for that is merely the other side of the coin. In the spiritual realm, logical and illogical simply do not apply.

Each of us is an individual and so must develop our own method for getting a peek beyond logic. I can tell you how the process works for me and perhaps this will help you develop your own techniques.

I begin as I would with any physical problem. Using the logical mind, I examine the problem from all angles, thinking it through and trying for some insight which would lead to a solution. I turn it this way and that in my mind until I get as far as logic will take me. At this point the problem seems almost resolved— but not quite.

Now I go one more step. If I am truly receptive, logic falls away and a **knowing** takes its place. Using words, I can take you only as far as logic will go. Anything further must be developed between the hearers and their inner beings. Some find that holding the problem in mind at bedtime will lead to a clarifying dream.

Occasionally the entire process takes only a short time. Most spiritual concepts, however, require that you chew them over in your spare time at considerable length. The **knowing** is always worth the effort.

The entire thing should be stimulating and fun. In the spiritual realm, grim determination seldom produces results.

8

YOUR PERSONAL ENVIRONMENT

In whatever direction we look, we see physical objects. No less real are the ideas and emotions of the physical mind.

What we seldom realize is that each of them is an expression of a larger spiritual reality. They are the creations of our own focus.

Imagine that I pick up a pretty pebble and examine it. The pebble in my hand exists because I am focused on it. Unconsciously I am translating the spiritual equivalent of the pebble into the object in my hand.

Now I hand the pebble to you. As you examine it, it becomes the product of your focus. Is it the same pebble? Yes and no! It is a physical expression of the same spiritual idea, but since we are different individuals, each unique unto ourselves, your translation will not be identical to mine.

True enough, we can measure it, weigh it, describe it in the most minute detail and agree on every bit of this data, but the data itself is created anew in each mind of each physical self.

I say that the pebble is round and you agree. You describe the red streak running through it and I also see it. But is my perception of round the same as yours? Is your perception of red identical to mine?

We share this world—and yet it is not quite the same world. Each of us is rooted in our own spiritual being and translates the spiritual into the physical through our own unique focus.

As we look at the pebble together, there are actually two versions, each occupying the same space at the same time. We see our own translation of the pebble. The other is invisible—indeed, does not exist in our personal environment.[1]

This is, of course, simplified for clarity. There are wheels within wheels. The pebble exists, for instance, even to those who never have and never will observe its physical form.

Just as our cluster formed its own consciousness, we as physical selves share a collective physical consciousness operating by a sort of telepathy flowing constantly among us, just below the level of everyday thought. Our own private club, you might say. This makes all of us aware of any part of physical reality known to any other physical self.

The spiritual essence, of which the pebble is an expression, is also aware of itself. It has therefore an existence of its own, independent of our versions. Its own concept of its physical being occupies the same space and time as ours.

This all seems tricky and complicated to us only because we are approaching the limits of logic.

Once experienced as a **knowing**, it is perceived as a beautifully operating whole, like some metaphysical Swiss watch, each part performing its own independent function, yet meshing smoothly into the functions of all the other parts to become a splendidly organized reality.

Because each physical self has a unique focus, differing from the focus of any other, each nook and cranny of our reality is constantly being explored and the spiritual space expanded in myriad directions. Your own focus may be able to open a door which I cannot even perceive.

Each new idea conceived, each fresh creation of any soul in this or any other reality, opens new space for the expansion of the

---

1 Each of us lives in a personal environment that is the sum total of our interpretation of the spiritual into the physical. By this token our reality is multiplied by the number of physical selves that are now living, ever have lived, or ever will live. The general outline is agreed upon by our collective physical consciousness, but each fills in that outline with a different interpretation as dictated by their own unique personality and focus.

Creator's being and new realms in which new realities can be constructed.

As we add to the Creator's being, we add also to our own, for one is all and all are one.

Of all the infinite souls in all the infinite realities, there is no other identical to you or me. Your individuality is yours alone and can never be taken from you. Nothing, once created, can be uncreated.

Your physical mind may doubt this as you watch mighty civilizations crumble into dust. The physical aspects of these civilizations are but an expression of their spiritual aspects. As the spiritual reality grows, it surpasses the physical aspects, which no longer adequately express it. A new expression is created and the old one crumbles, but the larger reality exists and grows forever.

As physical selves, we were individualized when our cluster idea began to express itself physically. We forever remain a part of our larger soul, just as all that is, is forever a part of the Creator. As individuals, however, we are now aware of ourselves and have free will of our own.

Our feet have been set upon a path that has no end. Each goal attained opens our consciousness to a new, larger, and more glorious goal. Each ending becomes a new beginning.

Using the abundant energy flowing from the Creator through our own soul, we forever evolve into a greater, and still greater, being.

We are already, without being aware of it consciously, individualizing portions of ourselves. Any new idea conceived, if enough emotion is contained in it, exists and evolves forever. As it builds and adds to its being, so does it also add to ours, for it is forever a part of us.

Over a period of many years I have periodically found myself in a familiar landscape in my dreams. It began as simply an ocean beach. In my dream adventures I first added a pier jutting into the water. In subsequent visits I found shops on the piers selling all sorts of strange merchandise. Mountains, streams and farms grew. Lately buildings and streets, which seem to be growing into a large city, are in this land. The place is populated by many individuals, all created from my mind while dreaming.[2]

---

2 I am not entirely sure that this dream reality is all of my own creation. It may well be that other entities are working with me on this project unbeknownst to my physical self.

You may dismiss this as mere fantasy, but dreams, in their own realm, are as real as the earth on which we walk.

Recently I have encountered buildings which come as a surprise to me. I travel roads and cross bridges which I had no hand in constructing.

I return less frequently now, and when I do I am only a visitor. The land and its people have attained individuality and operate by their own free will. I no longer direct any growth but merely observe.

The energy which is their raw material flows from the Creator, but is channeled through my own larger being. Though their existence is not as substantial as our own, they have been started down the path.

I know that mine is not a unique experience for when I broach the subject, I find that many people have such dreams. A woman of my acquaintance has constructed a castle that is inhabited. It may well be the beginning of her own land.

All dream construction is not, of course, so detailed. The child who constructs a monster in its nightmares out of its own fears, and wakes screaming, has individualized that monster which now exists in its own realm.[3]

Certainly there was enough emotion to give impetus to that creation. The child did not expressly create a realm for the monster to live in, but one would be implied by its very characteristics. In its own realm the monster would not be monstrous but a normal inhabitant. Of course, such a rudimentary and instantaneous creation would be very limited indeed. The poor monster has a long road ahead of it.

There is another sort of quasi-creation which draws its substance from those who believe in it. This semi-being may gain its form from one individual but is more often a group creation. These have been termed thought forms.

As used here, the term "thought form" refers to a thought held so strongly in the mind of one or more individuals that it becomes apparent to one or more of the physical senses.

When belief wanes, the strength of the thought form dwindles but never dissipates entirely. It never attains true individuality or free will. It often has the appearance of great strength, but this is misleading. Since it gains its power through belief, it has none over

---

3 At the same time, the child has brought itself back into emotional balance by externalizing its excess fear, discharging it into the being of the monster.

unbelievers, and even its power over its adherents is illusory.[4]

Fairies, leprechauns and other "little people" from cultures around the world are such thought forms. In ancient times, belief in fairies was so strong that they were often visible. The Irish banshee is still heard in remote parts of that land. As Christianity displaced the old nature worship, the thought forms dwindled until they became merely colorful tales of folklore.

Thought forms with the strength to become apparent to the senses are rare in our civilization. We pay little attention to what cannot be weighed and measured.

Rather than growing into greater being, thought forms wax and wane as belief in them comes and goes. They never grow beyond the powers that belief gives them.

We are meant to be much more aware of this spiritual activity than we are.

Our physical mind is based in a physical organ—the brain. Being physical, the brain can experience only physical things, flesh and matter. It may speculate on our spiritual activities, but cannot experience them directly. Most of us spend virtually all our time in this reality focused in the physical mind. The thought of removing the focus from the brain and focusing for a time in the spiritual mind frightens us. We fear that our bodies and brains will fail to function without our constant attention.

We forget that our bodies are created, nurtured and sustained by *Hiyei Hiyasu*, Mother of All, the Earth who has given them an inborn wisdom of their own.

I take a walk down a country lane. As I walk, I think of many things. I daydream and look at the clouds overhead. I pay little attention to my body and yet it trudges obediently down the road, maintaining its balance and placing one foot before the other. Even if I concentrate on my walking, I don't really know how I do it. I cannot trace the hundreds of precise muscle adjustments involved in every step. I think "walk" and the body walks. I think "stop" and the walking ceases. What a marvelous vehicle our Mother has provided us with!

---

4 Conjuring of demons is usually accomplished by ritual designed to feed emotion into a thought form. Many of these so-called demons are long dormant, but any of them may be resurrected with sufficient belief and strong emotion. The conjurer usually seeks to gain power from the demon—an exercise in futility for, ironically, it is the other way around.

Eat some food and your conscious awareness of it ends as soon as it is swallowed. With no help from us, the body processes the food, breaking it down into its elements and providing each cell with precisely the elements it needs to function properly.

Your body is well-equipped to care for itself as you shift your focus to the spiritual mind for a time. A line of communication always remains and your brain can instantly call your attention to a physical emergency.

This is not to say that we should spend **all** of our time in the spiritual mind. To do so would throw us out of balance in the other direction. We are, after all, the eyes and ears of our soul in physical reality.

Our efficiency at this task cannot help but improve, however, if we familiarize ourselves with our subject. It is difficult to be in harmony with a spiritual reality that we have never experienced.

As we create and grow, so do we add to the being of the Creator, and the Creator to our being. The time will certainly come when our individual spiritual being becomes too great to remain in the reality which we presently occupy. Even now only a portion of our soul will "fit." The greater part of us exists outside the physical realm.

Expanding forever, each of us will become one day beings greater than we can conceive of in the physical mind. We, like the Creator, exist and grow for all eternity.

SPIRITUAL HARMONY
IN PHYSICAL LIFE

Our spiritual life is organized along a great many simultaneous lines. Our awareness of one over the other depends on our focus at the time.

The primary line of focus in physical reality has already been set forth. Our physical self, though it has its own soul, is also part of the greater soul from which our individuality emerged. Our greater soul is part of the collective soul shared with our soul mates. The collective soul, in turn, is part of the Creator's being. This line of focus emerged when we were individualized and will remain so long as physical reality exists.

As we work and create in different areas of our spiritual life, different lines come in and out of focus. We have already seen how our consciousness became part of a cluster consciousness. Our physical selves also share a consciousness whose role is overall organization of physical reality.

This tale illustrates one way in which a new consciousness may come about.

Expansion

On the very top of a rocky hill is a pine tree. It has found a small pocket of soil in which to grow. Nothing grew on this hill till the pine burst from its seed.

Carefully, for many years, it has searched for tiny cracks into which its smallest roots could slip. As they pressed against the rock, other tiny cracks appeared, into which other roots could slip.

Water seeped into these cracks and froze in the winter, expanding them further. Wind blew dust into the cracks and they slowly filled with soil. After many years of labor by the tree there were small veins of soil running through what had been solid rock.

The seeds of trees and bushes growing around the hill found their way into the veins of soil where they continued the work started by the pine. The pine also dropped seeds about itself and many of them were able to sprout where no tree could have before the pine came to the hill.

Grasses and herbs grew about the trees, catching particles of dust and bits of leaves, building soil which slowly covered the bare stone.

Birds came to nest in the trees and squirrels feasted on acorns and pine nuts. Rabbits ate the grasses and herbs. Earthworms and insects worked in the soil, enriching it so that more green things could grow.

If you go to this hill now you will see it clothed top to bottom with growing plants. Only here and there does a bit of stone show. Birds will sing around you and small animals will scurry about. It is a busy place where *Hiyei Hiyasu* has borne many children.

So does your soul search out barren places of the spirit where it may insert the roots of consciousness.

As this space expands, it will attract other souls who will work to make this a fertile place where the seeds of new ideas may grow into fine new realities to expand the being of the Creator and all who participate.

I tell you now. Perceive the work of your soul and participate as it creates new space and expands into it. What was once barren will grow into a place rich in consciousness, in which both you and your soul will find joy.

As souls participate in mutual **knowing** (their form of communication), ideas and possibilities for expansion of spiritual space are often perceived. This perception attracts other souls whose individual traits interest them in the possible project. Interaction of the various souls invariably produces a group consciousness which is able to effectively focus the energy in order to bring the idea into reality.

All of us are constantly contributing to many projects without the conscious awareness of the physical mind. These are undertaken in both the waking and dreaming states. The extent of our participation may range from long term in some cases to a mere dipping in and out in others, as our individual personality leads us. We often monitor projects without participating in them.

There is nothing to keep you from awareness of these activities except your own focus. Once you learn to focus in the spiritual mind, you will become aware of many such undertakings. Some of them are even now shown to you in your dreams. Like your dreams, however, many of them can be shown to you only in symbols, for the words of ordinary thought are inadequate to express them.

The physical mind in which we live our everyday lives is very specialized. It was constructed to be highly efficient in physical expression. To perceive spiritual matters you must focus in the spiritual mind.

Other projects, once perceived, can be quite well understood in the physical mind. The book which I am now writing is one such project of my own. Obviously I am receiving a great deal of cooperation from other spiritual entities. Perception of these hitherto unconscious activities will result in greater harmony with our inner being, for knowledge is indeed power— power for further expansion of our own and the Creator's being.

The more power you learn to use effectively, the more will be available to you. Your life will become more joyous and your days fuller.

On the physical level, we must keep in mind that we are here to express the spiritual in flesh and matter. We are the focus of our soul in physical reality. I repeat this many times for, in our everyday activity, this is the key to the joyful life we all wish for ourselves.

Remembering that our soul can apply itself only where we focus, we must be alert to focus on solutions rather than problems. When our vision is clear, we see that evil is not something in its own right, but the lack of something— namely, harmony.

The Nanina concept of *korak* (which, remember, is disharmony between our physical and spiritual being) is much nearer the truth. When we are in harmony, the energy flows smoothly and effortlessly through us, forming a reality full of peace and abundance.

When we are in *korak*, we are like a river full of rocks and snags. The energy will flow but, like the water in the river, it will foam and roil, tumbling in all sorts of unpredictable directions.

We often perceive the troubles in our lives as being imposed upon us by some outside force. The truth is that the trouble arises within us, fueled by our *korak*. Because of our misdirected focus, energy is brought into our personal environment in an undesirable form. We see the "evils" about us and never recognize them as our own creations.

The programs directed by our government are a prime example of misdirected focus.

It is fashionable to be cynical about the men and women who work in our government, but these programs are, for the most part, headed by men and women of high ideals and staffed by workers quite sincere in their desire to solve the particular problem at hand. Yet, in spite of their untiring efforts, the problem usually worsens.

The usual first step of these agencies is a detailed study of the problem, paying little attention at this point to the solutions. The concentration of the attention of all these dedicated people is unfortunately focusing a great deal of energy into the problem they think they are fighting. The result is like trying to drown a fire with gasoline.

We know very well what the problems are in our lives. We need no detailed study to understand them. Our focus must be on solutions.

The person who feeds poverty with their hate of it only assures the continuation of that poverty. Since the attention is focused on the problem, that is where the energy enters.

If you wish to eliminate poverty in your own life, focus on abundance and share with all about you, no strings attached. Poverty is thus weakened, and enough people doing so could eliminate it in the physical world.

When first bringing ourselves back into harmony, we must remember that we bound ourselves by certain laws when creating physical reality. One of these laws is that time is perceived as flowing in a straight line, and in only one direction. We experience this as past, present and future.

Any action taken, whether in or out of harmony, thus requires the passage of time before affecting our personal environment.

We may decide to focus on abundance today, only to face an unexpected expense tomorrow. At that point, many will decide it doesn't work and give it up.

The first step in improving our personal environment is admittedly the most difficult.

We must continue to focus on, and believe in, that which we wish to bring about, while the evidence of our physical sense is often to the contrary.

Settle for a gradual improvement. You will accept a cabbage with a torn leaf. How can you demand immediate perfection in your spiritual harmony?

Your most powerful tool in holding this focus is proper use of emotion. Feed strong emotion into the solution and, insofar as possible, deny emotion of any kind to the problem itself.

You must, however, **not** struggle against such emotion. To do so is to fall into the same old trap. You are once again focusing on, and feeding strength to, the problem.

You must allow energy to flow through and dissipate without a specific focus. Take your focus a step back from the physical mind—not quite into the spiritual mind but into a sort of holding position between. Observe the emotion dispassionately, as though it were happening to someone else—sort of like a spiritual matador allowing the bull of emotion to pass within inches of you without disturbing a hair of your head. Soon enough it will lose its momentum without your participation in it.

I cannot, through use of words, teach you to do this any more than I can teach you to ride a bicycle by explaining it. You must climb on and, after a suitable number of bruises, *voilá!* Down the road you go.

The emotions you are feeding into the solution should, on the other hand, be participated in to the fullest extent. Participate in them joyfully, fully expecting them to bring about the desired result.

The unexpected expense mentioned above must, of course, be dealt with, but if we do so with much weeping and wailing and gnashing of teeth, if we take an attitude of "Everything happens to me," we set ourselves up for another round of problems. Deal with it matter-of-factly, put it into the past and go on focusing on harmony.

Gradually your new focus will manifest itself. With each change for the better, your focus will become easier to hold. Be prepared for a rough spot in the road here and there. The results of past *korak* sometimes take a considerable time to manifest themselves.

What you are trying to eventually attain is a smooth flow in your life. In the beginning you may find it necessary to concentrate on solutions to problems one by one as detailed above.

As you gradually gain harmony between your physical and spiritual self, and thus with all above them, you will not have to puzzle out solutions at all. The proper actions will take place and problems begin to dissolve almost automatically.

Your own attitude is of prime importance. You must cultivate a frame of mind in which you confidently expect the proper results.

Focusing on harmony does not mean to exert all your force, straining to achieve it. Such strain will, of itself, upset the very harmony you seek. A relaxed, confident expectancy is the key to results.

When this smoothness is interrupted, as it will be from time to time, be alert to discern the true intentions of your soul. It may indeed be a problem caused by wrong focus. It may, however, be a way of calling your attention to an opportunity to expand your being. (See the tale "Opportunity" in Chapter Four.)

Those who have studied Oriental religions may believe that they recognize *korak* as the *karma* of Buddhist and certain other religions. There are some important differences between them.

As already mentioned, there was neither dogma nor formal religion in Nanina society. Each person was allowed his or her personal beliefs, but there was much discussion and insistence on refining and testing one's beliefs through **knowing**. This resulted in a more or less general agreement on many important spiritual concepts.

Karma

For those unfamiliar with the doctrine of *karma*, I will give a necessarily brief explanation.[1]

Karma may be thought of as a sort of celestial bookkeeping. Each negative action creates a debt which must be canceled by an equal or greater positive action. In some sects, suffering or punishment may substitute to cancel the debt. The effects of negative and

---

[1] This is by no means meant to be a complete explanation of *karma*. A book longer than this one could easily be written on this doctrine, and many excellent ones have been. Any large public library can supply you with several.

positive actions are carried from one reincarnation to the next till they are eventually balanced.

When one's spiritual books are in perfect order, one enters Nirvana, a blissful state of losing one's identity, being absorbed into the Godhead.

In the Nanina concept of *korak*, no balancing of action is necessary. It is simply a matter of being in harmony, which is pleasant, or out of harmony, which is not.

Unlike *karma*, *korak* does not apply to the larger soul. It is impossible to be out of harmony with your soul except on the physical level. No debts are carried over. If there is to be another physical life, it will begin in harmony.[2]

Guilt

A word about guilt may be appropriate here. This concept is so ever present in our society that we build religions on it, weave it into our legal system, base a great deal of our advertising on it and use it as a club to beat one another and our own children into submission.

Our mental institutions overflow with people so obsessed with feelings of guilt that they have no energy left for anything else.

A sizable portion of our population pump their brains full of alcohol, heroin, cocaine, anything to momentarily escape the oppressive feelings of worthlessness engendered by guilt.

So all-pervasive is it that it might almost be regarded as a cornerstone of our civilization.

We hear in some of our churches that we are born guilty and live our lives in sin. Born guilty? This is the most ridiculous idea imaginable. These people are professing belief in a God who purposely builds flawed creatures and then punishes them for those flaws. The guilty party in such an arrangement would be the sadistic God responsible.

---

[2] Most Nanina believed that at the end of our physical life we are free to go in whatever direction we perceive as best for growth in being. Some may choose to return to physical reality while others choose a different path. Each of us is unique and so is the path we choose to follow.

The emotion of guilt was never meant to be as all powerful as we have made it through our wrong focus. In its natural form the emotion is quite simple and positive.

We have seen why an action leading to a state of *korak* takes time to show a result in this reality. The function of guilt is to alert us, before the result manifests itself, to the fact that a wrong action has been taken and that we are in danger of losing our harmony. We may then take whatever action is possible to correct the error and avoid repeating the action.

Once we have recognized this and taken whatever steps are open to us, guilt should dissipate as easily and completely as any other emotion.

10

PHYSICAL AND
EMOTIONAL HEALTH AND
BIRTH DEFECTS

In order to fully participate and create in physical reality it is necessary to have physical expressions of ourselves. These expressions are the bodies which we wear. Our body is a life-form produced by *Hiyei Hiyasu*, Mother of All, the Earth, under the guidance of our cluster consciousness, and with the participation of the physical self who will inhabit it.

Our Mother the Earth has given the body an indwelling wisdom of its own. It is a constantly renewing life-form, each day shedding countless worn-out and dead cells in untold numbers and replacing them with new ones. In a very real sense you no longer wear the same body you wore only a few years ago, yet you have a sense of continuity. At no one point can you detect this constant change, though if you compare a picture of yourself taken ten years ago with your present appearance, the change may be striking.

Reflect for a moment on the marvelous efficiency of your body. No machine ever built can approach it. You can fuel it with a sandwich and a glass of milk, then spend three or four hours spading a garden. An equivalent amount of fuel would hardly be enough to start most machines.

Using the same hands and arms, you can thread a needle and swing a sledgehammer. With the same feet and legs you can walk a mile, dance a jig and climb a ladder.

It would take a thousand or more machines to perform the tasks your body does so easily, and a new one would have to be constructed each time you learned a new skill.

Most internal functions of your body are performed without the participation of your physical mind. Were it necessary to constantly monitor each organ, keeping all in balance and functioning properly, you would have time for little else. The state of your body, both internal and external, is a reflection of your spiritual being in physical reality.

The above refers, of course, to those who were born into healthy bodies which function properly. The case of those whose health is poor at birth, or with bodily impairment in one area or another, will be dealt with later in this chapter.

Disharmony with our spiritual being will be reflected on the physical level, sometimes in our personal environment but often in the functioning of our bodies.

The tendency of our bodies is to maintain themselves in health at all times. This tendency is often interrupted, however, by a disruption of the harmony between our spiritual and physical elements. As an expression of our spiritual self, the body will reflect this disharmony as illness. The next tale points out another possible cause of illness.

Wisdom

High in a tree a pair of newly mature birds is building a nest. Patiently they search the area about them. They begin with twigs and dry pine needles, wedging them into place in the branches. They weave these tightly together with grass and fiber. When the nest is strong and bound tightly into place, they line it with fluff from ripe cattail reeds.

Now they have a fine home in which to raise the young birds, sheltered from rain by the leaves above, securely tied so it will not be blown apart, soft and comfortable for the babies' tender skins.

In a dry, dark hollow place within the same tree a new swarm of bees has moved in. They scour the hollow, tearing off rotted bits of wood and throwing them outside till the lining of the hollow is firm and sound. They make wax and build the first combs in precisely the right place. They gather nectar and make honey to fill the combs. The queen lays eggs in other combs and the rearing of new bees begins. It is a fine, dry, happy home.

In the small stream below the tree a newly mated pair of beavers is building a dam. They have chosen carefully. It is a place where a small dam will flood a large area. Each stick is wedged into just the right place and clay is packed between and around the sticks.

As the dam rises, the water rises with it and soon the beavers are able to build a comfortable lodge in the center of a fine new pond, the door deep below the water for safety.

Yet—how were the birds able to build a nest the same as those built by all other members of their tribe? They had never built a nest before, or even seen one built.

The bees were given no lessons in preparing a new hive before leaving the old one. The beavers had no rawhide with pictures on it showing the steps in damming a stream.

Each of these creatures proceeded with their task trusting their own nature in the knowledge that *Hiyei Hiyasu* would give them the guidance necessary. The Mother of All sees to it that all her children have whatever knowledge is needed in order for each to live the life intended for it.

Had the birds tried to build a dam, they would have muddied their feathers till they could not fly. Had the beavers tried to build a nest, they would have fallen from the branches. Had the bees built a nest in the open, they would have been robbed of their honey. The result would have been turmoil with nothing accomplished.

So is your physical body a child of *Hiyei Hiyasu*, and she will not fail to give it wisdom. If you cut your finger, it needs no instruction in healing. No one taught your heart to beat or eyes to see.

I tell you now. Trust the wisdom of your body. Do not interfere in its physical workings. Allow it freedom to do what it does so well. Do not send beavers to climb trees or birds to flounder in the mud.

Every doctor is familiar with patients who monitor each heartbeat, fleeing to them in panic at the slightest irregularity.

Our hearts beat constantly, yet there are flutterings or even occasional missed beats. It is of no consequence— merely the heart adjusting itself to the body's needs. Similar irregularities can be detected in many other bodily functions.

Constant monitoring sends confusing messages to the organ in question, causing further disruption in its functioning till it is thrown out of its natural rhythm.

Too often we concentrate on each little ache and pain, feeding energy into our ailments. Faithful servant that it is, our body will interpret this focusing of energy as a desire to maintain or increase the problem rather than correct it and will act accordingly. Our focus should be on health and our attitude one of confident expectancy of well-being.

In some cases, however, an illness may actually be beneficial, serving to correct an imbalance in the body, reflecting a correction that is being made on the spiritual level. Such illnesses will never be chronic.

If the body is left free to maintain itself and we are reasonably in harmony with our souls, then germs, viruses and other disease organisms will seldom be able to invade it.

Do not interpret this as an injunction to abandon the medical profession. So long as the system of beliefs which creates your personal environment includes a belief in modern medicine, and so long as imbalances occur, the services of a doctor may be needed from time to time.

If, however, you find yourself getting over one illness only to fall into another, and spending an inordinate amount of time in the doctor's office or hospital, perhaps it is time you examined your spiritual life.

I cannot help thinking that the practice of modern medicine would be much improved by the adoption of the way of Nanina healers. Medicine was accompanied by spiritual and psychological counseling in order to restore the individual to harmony.

This practice is used to this day by Mexican *curanderos* and such Indians as the Navaho who have managed to preserve many of the old ways.

Internally your body is self-sustaining but any dealings between it and the outer world are directed by your physical consciousness.

Your body tells you when it is hungry but cannot eat till you direct it to do so. It cannot don clothes when cold, exercise itself or take any other external action except under your direction.

In a manner of speaking, you and your body are partners so long as you inhabit physical reality. It cannot long function when you have left it permanently, and you cannot remain physical without it.

As the senior partner in this arrangement, you must see that the body has what it needs from the physical world. The proper amount of rest and exercise, fresh air, clean water and a good diet are for you to provide. Your body is amazingly adaptable, but even the best body cannot long maintain itself if grossly overworked, underexercised or fed a steady diet of junk food.

Those who have been born with a debilitating disease or a body unable to function in one area or another may take comfort in the knowledge that there is indeed a reason.

Our bodies were carefully chosen by us prior to donning them. In a sense, you might say that they were built to our specifications. At first glance it may seem foolish indeed to enter physical reality in an imperfect body when we could have had a fine, healthy one.

In our physical world it is sometimes difficult to remember that we are spiritual beings with a physical expression rather than the other way around, and that we constantly grow into greater being.

In a purely spiritual state, as we were prior to entering the physical realm, this is realized more clearly. We are able to perceive our individuality with strengths and weaknesses without physical distraction. We are more aware of where we are and where we wish to go.

This is put, of course, in terms understandable to the physical mind. There are many factors at work, and the physical mind can perceive only part of the process.

Know this. The body you wear is the one **you** chose of your own free will and for your own reasons. As a unique individual, with your own unique focus, you may have had any number of excellent reasons for doing so.

Before commenting further, perhaps Storyteller's next tale will help clarify the matter.

Crystals

A mother has brought her child to Plant-Talking Woman. The child has spells when it is unable to breathe properly. Exposed to dust or smoke, the child struggles and wheezes, unable to draw sufficient air into its lungs. Both the child and mother are frightened.

Plant-Talking Woman has seen this illness before and knows the medicine needed. She puts toasted grain and dried berries into her pack, along with sharp scrapers and soft deerskin for wrapping the medicine, and sets out for a mountain where pine trees grow.

At the base of the mountain are many pines with long straight trunks. They are beautiful as they dance in the wind, their needles singing their joy in every gust. Plant-Talking Woman admires their supple grace and feels their joy, but they are not what she seeks.

Farther up the mountains she finds pines of a different nature. They are more exposed and have grown slower. Their large sturdy trunks grow from roots which clasp the earth in a mighty grip. Their trunks hardly bend in the gusts of wind. Their broad crowns sing a song of pride in their rugged well-being. She stands for a time, participating in their pride and feeling the energy which flows so freely within them, then passes onward. They do not have what she needs.

For three days she climbs upward, clambering over gullies and crossing rock ledges, the trees becoming fewer as she labors up the mountains.

Finally she reaches the peak. Among the rocks stands a single stunted pine, twisted and gnarled by the harsh wind which buffets it, the bark worn away on the windward side by sand flung against it. For countless ages it has clung to its rocky crag, struggling for each inch of growth, sometimes spending many years producing one branch, only to have it torn away in a single storm. In its struggles it has produced so little growth that Plant-Talking Woman can stand on tiptoe and reach the very top of it.

She kneels facing it, both palms flat against the trunk, merging her consciousness with that of the misshapen tree so that it will know what she needs of it.

She takes a pouch of soft, rich earth scooped at the base of the mountain and packs it carefully between the rocks at the base of the trunk as a token of respect for the tree's place in the being of *Hiyei Hiyasu* and of the Creator.

Standing, she searches the scars and wounds upon the tree until she finds several covered by crystals formed by the sap oozed to seal off the damage. These hurts are almost healed and she carefully scrapes away as many of the crystals as she can without exposing the wound or harming the tree. One last time, she caresses the tree with her hand, then turns and starts back down the mountain.

Placed in boiling water the crystals will form a vapor which the child can breathe in to open its lungs and ease the ailment.

Only a pine which must struggle for survival and conserve each drop of sap can produce such crystals. A vigorous pine further down the hill will cover a wound with a copious flow of sap, full of pine tar and useless in a case such as this.

So do the struggles caused by a body lacking in some respect produce crystals of wisdom. Properly used, these crystals may produce a healing and growth of the spiritual

being which could never occur in a more vigorous body.

I tell you now. Search within the spiritual mind that you **know**. Offer up these crystals that your being may be strengthened. What is perceived as weakness in physical existence often produces great strength in spiritual being.[1]

Your larger self is more aware of its being than is possible at the physical level. On this higher plane you are aware of your growth in one area and lack of it in another. You know where experience must be gained and energy focused in order to maintain balance and evolve into greater being. You understand yourself and your nature and do not seek to hide your weaknesses from yourself as the physical self often does.

---

[1] Storyteller's love and admiration for Plant-Talking Woman are very apparent in this tale. In all his tales, only Plant-Talking Woman is given a name.

Not only your body but all circumstances of your birth— such as time, location, vigor or lack of it, and many other factors— are carefully considered prior to entering physical life.

Even your potential parents are chosen with great care. Will you be born to famous people who help form the destinies of great civilizations or be the child of a beggar? Will you be raised in great luxury or search in trash cans for a crust of bread? Would your growth be best served as male or female?

Knowing that your perception of spiritual tasks will dim at physical birth, these factors and many others are carefully woven together to incline the physical self toward the life that would best serve your higher purpose. Perhaps to be born blind and impoverished would best focus your life on the areas that will direct growth where it is needed.

Allow me to set up a simple example. Suppose a larger self perceives that growth is necessary on an intellectual level. Aware of its own individuality, it knows that it has already explored physical reality as a great athlete in a strong, healthy body. Its memory of, and pride in, its accomplishment will be contained in the personality of the physical self, and if that self is born into a strong, vigorous body, its tendency may well be to reenter the world of sports and try to recapture the joy and satisfaction it found there.

This area has already been explored and reflected in the growth of being.

The larger self may therefore conclude that it is necessary to limit this tendency by being born into a body with crippled legs. In order to point the physical self in the right direction, it may choose a college professor married to an outstanding mathematician as parents and a time and place where mental accomplishments are highly honored.[2]

The crippled legs, which appear in physical reality as a weakness, are now seen to be an asset which will produce a fulfilling life and contribute to growth in spiritual being.

A life as a sports hero would seem in physical life to be a

---

[2] At the risk of being redundant, I must once again point out what is so easily forgotten. Your higher and physical selves are part of one individual who is **you**. The apparent division is a device which exists only in our particular reality for the purpose of allowing the physical self better to focus and create in flesh and matter. Once free of physical distraction, the separation dissolves.

wonderful accomplishment but would actually be wasted in covering ground already explored, contributing little or nothing to spiritual growth and leaving the physical self feeling vaguely discontented without knowing why.

Of course it is not likely to be as simple as this example. As much growth as possible will be attempted by the higher self, tying up a loose end here, breaking new ground there.[3] Each entity has its own unique personality and focus, and each path to greater being differs.

In order to understand the purpose of your higher self you must learn to sometimes focus in the spiritual mind and examine your own soul till a **knowing** takes place within you.

---

[3] Some, for instance, are born with diseases of the nervous system which do not show up for a number of years after birth. This might allow the physical self to live the first part of life in an apparently healthy body, then slowly shift the focus as the body becomes progressively handicapped.

THE MEANING AND FUNCTION
OF AGING

Because we have used a limited aspect of time as an important part of the framework on which our reality is based, we see our lives in a linear fashion.

We see ourselves as coming into existence at birth, passing through adolescence, adulthood, middle and old age, and leaving physical reality at death.

On a higher plane our lives existed, in essence, from the beginning of the idea which blossomed into our reality.

I hasten to add that this does not endorse fatalism, for no aspect of our lives is preordained or "finished," in the sense that change or refinement is impossible. This is no less true of the past than of the future.

It may aid the physical mind to grasp this idea if we think of our reality as a grand tapestry with both physical and spiritual elements intermingled. Our lives are woven into, and become part of, the design. Indeed, the entire tapestry consists of the intermingled lives and actions of all the souls and physical selves in our cluster (which, you will remember, is comprised of all the selves who will ever participate in physical life).

Unlike an earthly tapestry, however, this one is fluid. The design is ever-changing as we add to it and refine those additions. Energy from the Creator is channeled through us and becomes whatever we shape it into. As we shape this energy, it becomes part of the design and is added to the being of the Creator. The overall pattern was chosen by us at the beginning of time, but the refinements in design are woven by us as we live. The simplest act on our part flows outward, like the ripples of a pebble tossed into a pond, and affects the entire tapestry.

Though we may at times catch a glimpse of the grand design, we have chosen to base our reality on linear time and so must live our lives accordingly while we are here.

Storyteller has something to say of our linear lives in the following tale.

Ages

An old man sits on the trunk of a fallen tree. Before him is a shallow clay pit, muddy water puddled at the bottom. In the midst of this sits a naked young boy who has only recently learned to walk.

Laughing, he splashes about, delighting in the feel of the slippery red clay. He squishes it between fingers and toes and rubs it into his hair. He even tastes it. With wild abandon he plays his game, rejoicing in this newfound delight.

Looking through his eyes and perceiving the joy in his heart, his soul shares his experiences and expands in his joy.

Watching as the boy slithers from one end of his mud hole to the other, the old man thinks it is a fine thing to be discovering the many joys of *Hiyei Hiyasu* for the first time. "I remember," says the old man, "I remember."

At the edge of the pit sits a girl, slightly older than the boy. By her side, drying in the sun, are a snake and a dog, modeled from clay. With great concentration, she works on the figure of a sleeping deer, using twigs for antlers.

She knows that her creations will be displayed in a place of honor on the family hearth and that this evening the people of neighboring hearths will come to admire and praise them.

Her soul shares her creation and tonight will perceive her pride. Her soul gains strength and being through this creation and pride.

Watching her, the old man thinks how good it is to use the eyes and hands and mind and learn to create. "I remember," murmurs the old man.

Looking toward the huts, he sees a woman kneeling before a slab of pine placed across two flat rocks. By her side is a basket of moist clay taken from the pit. He watches as she rolls the clay into long ropes as thick as her thumb, then coils them atop one another to form a pot, useful for holding food or water and for storing many things. With a moistened finger she rubs the coils into one another till the wall of the pot is even in thickness, then presses a row of fingerprints around the rim and scratches a design into it with a sharp stick. When the form pleases her eye and heart, she sets it aside to dry and starts another.

Beyond the huts the old man sees smoke rising as her man prepares a fire pit to bake the pots. Both the man and woman will feel great satisfaction as they dig the pots out of the ashes. Their pride will be great as they share them with others and feel their pleasure. Their souls will expand in this satisfaction and pride.

The old man thinks how wonderful it is to make a useful object and how fine it feels to share with others. "I remember," says the old man.

He has once done all these things and been fulfilled in them, but now he is troubled, for he is too old to do them anymore. It seems to him that all his tasks lie behind and nothing lies ahead.

Turning his eyes inward, he asks his soul what his task is to be, then smiles as a **knowing** takes place within him. "Ah!" he says, "To remember and to perceive the pattern which lies within the memories."

I tell you now. Though you are eternal, the body ages. Do those things which seem natural and good to you at whatever age you find yourself. Your soul will grow in the perception of tasks well done.

Though each of us is a unique individual and chooses our own path of growth and creation, our collective consciousness has agreed upon an overall pattern to our lives in order to avoid chaos in physical reality.

Storyteller's tale does not deal with infancy. Though it is, of course, the first stage of physical existence, little actual creation takes place at this point. You might think of this stage as one of indoctrination. An infant, though it has a physical form, is still focused to a large extent in the spiritual mind. It is in the process of becoming at home here.

It is no accident that an infant begins its transition from the spiritual to the physical in a body which contacts its environment at a barely functioning level. It needs time to adjust before being bombarded with all the physical stimuli which it will, at later stages of life, handle so blithely.

It would be ridiculous to take a native of Stone-Age New Guinea who had never seen a car, plunk him behind the wheel and expect him to drive us across town at rush hour. Consider how much more difficult it would be to operate a human body at full capacity in a world so filled with glorious distractions.

The task of the infant is to learn about the body in which it resides and to develop skill in its use.

In the foregoing tale, Storyteller points to the next stages of life and their meanings.

The child in the mud hole is experiencing the first stage of life after infancy. You may think of this as an age of exploration. He is exploring and interacting with the world about him. No longer content to merely lie and observe, he now takes an active role. He searches out new emotions, experiences and sensations. As he does so on a physical level, this exploration reflects itself in his spiritual being.

In a manner of speaking, he is setting up a line of communication between his physical and spiritual self. This metaphysical switchboard will be refined and elaborated up to the final stage of physical life.

A child of this age often has an inborn ability to harmonize with many collective minds. When examining a butterfly, he enters so deeply into its world that, in all but the purely physical sense, he **becomes** a butterfly. Perhaps in his own unique personal environment, even the physical is transformed.

He individualizes portions of himself into imaginary playmates. Some are merely thought forms while others may well evolve a true individuality and free will of their own.

On a physical level, the child is taking a sort of inventory of all the elements available to him in his creation. The clay pit has perhaps been explored by countless Nanina children before him, but each has contributed a unique focus to the perception of *Hiyei Hiyasu* and the Creator.

It is important here to note the attitude of the Nanina people. Knowing that he is being watched by the old man, and is therefore safe, they leave him to his delights. They know that a dunking in the nearest pond will wash off the mud before evening and see only that he is performing tasks appropriate to his age.

Place this scene in the modern world and imagine the outcome. A parent, having no understanding of what is actually occurring, is likely to burst on the scene with threats and perhaps physical punishment, hauling the child off to be scrubbed nice and clean.

The child will be burdened with guilt, feeling that he has done a shameful thing and will become more and more hesitant about such interactions till he no longer feels a part of the natural world about him. The rightful tasks of his age will be neglected and his spiritual growth stunted.

The young girl in this tale has entered the next age, the age of manipulation.[1] In this stage interaction continues (as it should throughout physical life), but now manipulation of the physical environment is added. For the first time creation in the material sense is experienced. Typically this is creation for its own sake.

---

[1] Of course, as in the apparent divisions of our being, there is no sharp delineation. One stage flows into the next and we often move back and forth. To illustrate this, Storyteller shared a memory with me at this point in the tale:

A young mother, discovering her child cavorting in the mud, impulsively tossed aside her skirt and joined in. The action was contagious and in a short time everyone in the hut group, from toddler to old folks, was happily slinging mud about, laughing and shouting. The Creator shared much joy that day.

Clay is formed into figures, not pots. Stones are laid out in pleasing patterns, not built up into hearths. The physical self thus develops its dexterity while at the same time learning the uses and limitations of the medium available.

A considerable number of physical selves have come here primarily to experience this stage, and many remain in it to the very end. Certainly this is a fascinating age with much experience and growth to be gained. Painters, sculptors, musicians, dancers and many other artists are immersed in a world of art for art's sake. Their lives are devoted to the creation of beauty and cultivation of the spiritual side of life.

The majority of us move on to the next age and spend the largest portion of our lives there. The man and woman in the tale illustrate what might be called the age of exploitation.[2] This age coincides with what, in modern society, is called the working life.

Manipulation of the physical world now takes on new orientation. Useful objects result from our creation (although ideally, beauty in these objects remains a strong consideration). We make, or in our society help to make, an almost endless number of things, from huge skyscrapers to tiny microchips. Those who drive a truck or repair the machinery of production contribute as surely as those whose hands actually touch these objects.

Discovering that our manipulation can produce objects which combine usefulness and beauty, and make our lives easier and more enjoyable, we find that we have opened a door which leads to a fascinating and almost boundless world— a world full of opportunity for growth in our being.

It is so easy, however, to be caught up in a world of "things," that we sometimes lose sight completely of our spiritual being. Distracted by our everyday activities we forget the larger spiritual reality which lies beyond the mask of the physical till only the physical seems real. Unless we can weigh and measure it, it is considered of no importance.

Blindfolded by this attitude, it is all but impossible to remain on the path of harmony. We find ourselves tangled in the brush of our *korak*. Our creations have side effects of ugliness, pollution

---

[2] Exploitation need not be a negative thing. All physical creation is here for our use and if exploited in harmony with its spiritual essence will refine and add to physical reality without bad side effects.

and ultimately war and strife. We find ourselves on shaky ground indeed.

Many who hear these words will find themselves in service jobs (sales, government or private clerical work, etc.) and may wonder how this applies to them.

All physical creation does not result in an object which can be seen. Ideas and emotions generated by the physical mind are quite as real as "things." It is, if anything, more important to build in harmony here.

Just as creation of a physical object in *korak* can result in pollution of air and water, so can ideas and emotion produced in *korak* pollute your personal environment and disrupt the harmony of our physical world.

Hold to the principle of harmony in all things and you cannot go far wrong.

12

OLD AGE, WHERE DO WE GO FROM HERE?

Perhaps the most misunderstood of all ages is the final one, the age of contemplation.

If we have lost our harmony during the preceding age of exploitation and think that only the physical is real, we all too often perceive the old as having outlived their usefulness since they no longer produce what can be seen with physical eyes.

Like the final act of a play, however, this age should draw all that has gone before into a cohesive whole, summing up an entire lifetime of creation and giving it meaning.

Unless we, like the old man in the previous tale, perceive the pattern of our life, the individual actions that have gone before stand alone with no relation to one another. It is as though we had woven many tapestries, each separate from the others— one showing only trees, another a bare mountain, a third a lake, and so on. Unless all are drawn together into one, we have no true picture, but only disjointed fragments. Only when they are joined and placed into proper relationship to one another does a picture emerge in the weaving.

It is the natural tendency of the old to examine their lives, seeing how one act affects the next and brings it forth until the picture is discerned.

This final act is a necessary one if the soul is to perceive its physical creation as a whole, for it can do so only through the memories of the physical mind.

As their minds wander down the old familiar paths woven as they lived their lives, they pause here and there at the crossroads and peer down the paths they did not take. What would their lives have been had they married a different person, raised their children differently, handled this situation or that in a different way?

Here is valuable information indeed for their souls. In peering down these unused paths they are calling the soul's attention to points at which subtle change and refinement of a past life are possible, for the past is no more set in stone than the future. With care, their soul may be able to effect a change without unduly altering the grand design of the overall tapestry of physical existence.

Those who have spent time with the aged are familiar with a common phenomena. The old often remember events, not as they actually happened, but as they now realize, as they should have. This is usually put down to a combination of wishful thinking and senility, but are they not, at least in their personal environment, altering these events?

Historians, archaeologists and some anthropologists devote their working lives to understanding the past. In the course of their work they often make discoveries which drastically alter the picture of past events. An ancient culture which had always been considered Stone Age may be discovered to have known the secret of bronze. One who had been considered a traitor may be discovered to have been working behind enemy lines, risking his life and sacrificing his reputation on his country's behalf.

Are these really old truths, only recently perceived? Perhaps. It is quite possible, however, that these are points at which paths had been altered, long after we consider the entities who walked those paths as dead and gone. Once the alteration is accepted by our collective consciousness, it **becomes** the truth.

Coupled to remembering in the final stage of physical existence is the preparation for a return to spiritual being.[1] Just as the infant is primarily focused in the spiritual mind, gradually shifting focus to the physical, so is the reverse true of the old.

There are as many ways of making this change of focus as there are individuals who enter this age. Those who have remained in harmony or brought themselves back to it, will usually accomplish a smooth transition with full awareness of what they are doing and why.

Those with less rapport with the soul will be led into it as well as the soul can manage. So important is this final phase that the soul will exert every effort on behalf of the physical self. If they stubbornly cling to physical focus, the larger soul may well dim the material senses. The eyes become less keen, the physical sense less perceptive. Their pleasure in the interaction of the physical self and the world about it thus becomes less intense. This is often enough to start them in the right direction.

If they have lost the ability consciously to focus in the spiritual mind, it may be necessary to do so through the subconscious. To those about them it will appear that their mind is wandering. They may well be in one place while thinking they are in another, perhaps where they spent their youth or early days of their marriage. Speaking to a son, they may mistake him for a husband; a sister may be perceived as their mother.

Those about them may, if they understand, help them to accept the task before them and aid them in bringing the process into the conscious mind.

To those who love them, this may be distressing to witness, but it is a truly important task they are performing, one which may well demand their entire concentration.

Many people in the final state will alternate between spiritual and physical focus. Their loved ones may say sadly, "One day she's fine and the next she doesn't even know who I am."

In the very last stages, the consciousness often leaves the body for relatively long periods with only the most tenuous connection as they loosen the bonds to the physical body in which they have resided for so many years. Once again those in harmony will

---

[1] Remember that we were individualized when our cluster idea became physical. We have always, of course, been primarily spiritual beings, but if this is our first physical life, we may not have experienced a purely spiritual existence **as an individual**.

understand what is happening to them while those in *korak* may be confused and upset.

When the self severs the final ties to the body, those in *korak* may be disoriented, not realizing that they are no longer physical. They may try, usually unsuccessfully, to communicate with those still physical. The period of disorientation will vary with the individual. They may waste much effort trying to focus in the physical mind. The physical mind, however, is based in the brain, a part of the body, and after death all ties to the body are severed.

By concentrating its focus toward the physical, the entity places itself in solitary confinement. Usually communication with the physical sphere is all but impossible, and even if managed will be tentative and unsatisfying.

At the same time, the spiritual entities surrounding such a disoriented individual will find themselves unable to contact the one whose attention is turned away from them. The confused individuals are unaware of the spiritual feast spread before them.

Sooner or later they will fall into such a state of desperation that they will cry out for help, thus changing focus despite themselves. Suddenly they will find themselves surrounded by loving help and no longer alone.

There are entities who spend a great deal of energy in helping such confused individuals out of their self-imposed dilemma. Some have been through this on their own death; some have never worn flesh; and still others are presently in the flesh but so balanced in harmony that they are quite at home in the spiritual realm. Many of the latter do this work either in the dream state or during meditation, often without the conscious knowledge of their physical mind.

These entities will guide the wayward till they learn to handle their spiritual environment. Depending on the individual involved and their state of harmony, any number of methods may be chosen. Sometimes the individual is able to participate in mutual **knowing**. In other cases the entities may take on the guise of wise men or women, or of loved ones who have gone before.[2] The purpose is to assist the individual in regaining harmony with a new spiritual existence.

---

[2] There is no attempt to deceive. This method is adopted in order to lead the individual into spiritual life with as little distress as possible. It frequently happens that loved ones who have gone before will return to aid in the process.

Often the individual is reluctant to abandon completely the familiar physical environment. Since energy is so easily molded in this state and no time lapse is necessary (linear time exists only in the physical state), s/he may construct a new body in the image of the old one. This body is not really physical but has the appearance of being so. The individuals may construct a house to live in and clothing and adornment to wear. Spirit guides may join in with constructions of their own till they can ease the individual into acceptance of his/her new being.

Sooner or later such individuals will realize the futility of their actions. Looking about for challenge, they will perceive their true nature. Now they will be receptive to the task which those in harmony accepted immediately. Joining with the larger soul, they will examine the past life from the spiritual perspective as they already have from the physical one. In a manner which seems peculiar to those of us in the physical reality, they receive the perceptions sent by themselves while still physical.

The progress made, as well as missed opportunities and possible paths for future growth, will become apparent.

The physical self becomes aware of itself as part of the soul, and the soul is part of it. A merging takes place but the physical self is **not** reabsorbed into the soul. Once individuality is attained, it can never be relinquished. This is the point at which subtle changes may be made in the physical life which has been lived, though these changes may appear at any suitable point in physical time.

After this examination, and when such changes are made as are possible without disruption of the tapestry being woven, the entity will have a fuller understanding of its own nature, and a solid basis for planning future development. Guidance is always available, but free will operates here as in the physical state.

Another physical life or entry into an entirely different reality may be chosen. Many will choose to develop in an entirely spiritual direction.

We have now entered as far as we can with logic and words. Only **knowing** can take us further.

Death is the end only of our present participation in physical reality. The restrictive laws adopted at birth are no longer binding on us. In the spiritual life, many areas which we had purposely blocked off open once again to us. Our oneness with the soul and the Creator are realized. Possibilities for growth are multiplied enormously and our true immortality is realized.

13

HOW NANINA CONCEPTS APPLY TO MODERN LIFE

Two words recur time and again in Storyteller's tales: joy and pride. They are the ultimate test of Nanina philosophy, for they gauge our life and how we conduct it. Let's examine these concepts from their point of view.

The Nanina have two variations on their word for joy. **Wish**tari with the accent at the beginning, means much the same as we use the word, a feeling of happiness which wells up till it fills our being.

Wishtari, with the accent at the end, means far more. Picture a joy so all-pervading that as your heart swells with it, the universe itself joins in till the very air tingles with it flowing out from you to all creation, even as it returns to you from it. At such times all physical reality seems to exist within your breast. All that you behold is part of you— and you of it. In this experience we glimpse the spiritual reality of our being. This feeling comes only in those rare times when our spiritual and physical elements are perfectly attuned.

Both states add to your being and that of the Creator. In the state of *wishtari*, however, since we are performing our function as perceivers of physical reality to perfection, the energy level is higher, and creation thus enhanced. Of course it is impossible to maintain this state constantly. It is doubtful that you could remain physical were you able to do so.

Once this state is experienced, it is never forgotten but becomes a beacon to light your way through the darkest times of your life.

The creation of the finest machine or grandest cathedral is a small thing compared to the creation of joy within ourselves and those around us. Of course we cannot create joy within others without first creating it within ourselves and we cannot do this without first bringing our physical selves into harmony with our spiritual beings.

When we behold a creation of our hands, minds and hearts which is finely tuned to its spiritual essence, so finely tuned that it fairly vibrates with beauty, vitality and a sense of rightness, how can we help but overflow with joy?

Once, years ago in Japan, I found myself walking down a narrow country road in the early morning. The sun was barely over the horizon and a fine mist hung over everything so that sound was muted and color softened.

There before me was a one-room farm cottage surrounded by pines. The frame was of cypress, unadorned by paint and weathered to a silvery gray. The walls were of the native red clay and had not been limed white as the finer Japanese homes were at the time. The peak of the roof rose steeply, thatched with straw. The ground around the house was bare earth, with only a small clump of moss here and there, packed tightly by the generations of feet that had trod upon it and swept clean. The faint smell of wood smoke in the air betokened the simple breakfast being prepared within. At one side a conical straw hat hung from the handle of a hand cart, testimony that the farmer was not wealthy enough, in material terms, to own an ox. In the courtyard a rooster and two hens scratched busily, the only living things in sight.

I stood rooted in the road, frozen by the absolute harmony and rightness of the scene before me. I felt tears of joy upon my face as my soul grew within me. Though my physical self soon continued onward, a part of my soul stands in that road forever. Bless you, farmer. Your gift of joy is a part of my soul for all eternity.

The pride of which Storyteller speaks so fondly is not the high-headed arrogance so often seen today. Such pride has only a momentary sweetness which quickly turns to ashes in the mouth. It is, rather, the pride which comes of knowing that we are unique, that we are an important part of the Creator, that we have a part to play that cannot be played by any other person who ever has lived or ever will live. Without our individual contribution, the tapestry of physical creation can never be completed.

It is pride in each tiny growth of the soul within us, knowing that creation is expanded because we exist. It is the pride which comes of giving freely of whatever we have and of beholding the joy generated by our gift, saying that nothing is owed. The giver has received more than he has given. Above all, it is the pride which fosters and cherishes the pride of all other living beings, knowing that their growth nourishes our own.

Why do we so seldom feel this joy and pride in our day? Certainly our present age is not entirely in error. Never before has there been such a flow of material goods, created in such a short time, with so little effort.

Though there have always been cultures, such as the Nanina, in which freedom of ideas have been encouraged, human history has never seen a time when freedom is available to so many (though, sadly, not to all). Even many Americans are unaware that democracy, as presently defined, came into existence for the first time with the creation of the U.S.A., barely more than two hundred years ago. We Americans live in the oldest democracy on Earth.

Paradoxically, it is this very freedom and productivity which has led to our present dilemma. We have accomplished so much, so fast, that we are dazzled by our own creations. In the frantic pace of modern life, many have lost track of the spiritual aspects.

The Nanina were, perhaps as no people before or since, uniquely attuned to their own spiritual essence and to that essence in all things. We cannot, however, simply lift their culture in one piece and adopt it. Ours is a thickly populated world with problems they never faced.

When we examine their ideas on the nature of physical reality, therefore, it comes as a surprise how well they illuminate and suggest new answers to those problems.

The Nanina teach that physical objects are the product of our focus. All physical things are an expression of their spiritual essence. The degree of harmony in this expression is commensurate with our degree of harmony as we generate that focus.

Our society has concentrated on physical creation with no regard to consequences. If an object cannot be created without pollution, then the environment must be sacrificed. The Nanina would answer that if an object produces pollution or disruption of nature, then the object is not a faithful expression of its spiritual essence.

It hardly occurs to us to question that production is most efficient if done on a large scale. Thousands of plastic cereal bowls roll off the line in the same time a potter would need to produce a dozen or so from clay. The fact that the clay bowl bears the imprint of the potter and is not identical to any other bowl ever made is not considered important. The plastic bowl is cheaper and just as good— or is it?

It is hard to imagine the plastic factory workers looking forward to the day's work or feeling the inner satisfaction of the potter as the clay takes shape under one's hand. True, the plastic bowl may cost a dollar whereas the clay bowl costs five. Consider this fact, however: the plastic bowl is not intended to last very long. It soon becomes shabby and is thrown away to add to pollution of the environment (not to mention the pollution when it was created). This rapid loss of whatever beauty it had is proof of its lack of harmony. The clay bowl will last virtually forever if not broken. Museums contain many clay bowls thousands of years old which are still as attractive and serviceable as the day they were made. A clay bowl in daily use may last several generations before being broken. We have all seen such bowls.

Let us consider the life of a plastic bowl as one year and a clay bowl as twenty. In those twenty years of buying plastic bowls you have spent the equivalent price of four clay bowls and you still have only one characterless bowl of no significant emotional value. The clay bowl is now a family heirloom. It is a warm feeling to see your child eating from the same bowl you used as a youngster. Can we put a price on that?

Is then, the ugly, smelly plastic factory more efficient than the potter working quietly at her wheel? It would seem not. Many other things which we consider as unpleasant but necessary do not stand up to closer inspection.

How do we set about the huge task of bringing our civilization back into harmony? The only possible place to start is within ourselves. If we bring ourselves into harmony, so also will our creations be.

As an individual, your path to inner harmony will not be the same as mine or anyone else's, but each can contribute to harmony in society.

As you search for harmony, you will often find that others of like mind will be drawn to you. Such groups will accelerate your development because several in mutual harmony will develop a group consciousness which is able to draw and focus energy with greater efficiency than the same number of persons living alone.

There are already many such groups, to a large extent unaware of one another on the physical level, each working along different paths, each influencing the tapestry of physical existence. When sufficient groups have formed, a merging will take place. Each will find their path merging with the others and augmenting the overall effort.

Trust and follow the urging of your inner self. Like the Nanina, however, submit each insight to the test of **knowing**. Be cautious in making drastic changes in your life till you are sure that you know what you know. Talk your insights over with others in your group, but— above all— trust your inner self.

As a physical self, limited to a linear time, there is but one point at which you can effectively influence physical reality and that is the point at which you find yourself. One entity in harmony can influence physical reality far more than a great number in *korak*, who will be pulling in all directions.

It may seem paradoxical that I tell you that you can change the world by bringing your focus down to your personal environment, but remember that the world within is infinitely greater and more powerful than all physical creation, which exists only as an expression of the inner you. As a part of the Creator, all knowledge exists within your being.

Now I give you a word of power. The same word spoken to me by Storyteller in the beginning. It has made my life more than I could have imagined a few years ago. ***Remember!***

14

THE WRITING OF THIS BOOK

Who really wrote this book? My name is on the cover, but when I sort through it, I find great difficulty in separating my own words and thoughts from those of Storyteller and the collective consciousness of the Nanina people.

The tales, of course, are pure Storyteller and I changed not a word except at his direction.

Many of the early chapters consist of the tales of Storyteller, followed by my comments upon them, but even here I could feel a guiding hand. In the later chapters, the tales became fewer as the material delved deeper into spiritual matters. Much of the material in these later chapters came to me as a **knowing** and I was often sore pressed to find words to express it.

At other times the words would pour into my head as fast as I could write them down, and at these times a curious thing would occur. I would be scribbling along, congratulating myself at the progress I was making, when I would suddenly realize that the ideas I was writing of were new to me and I didn't really understand them at all. Only after studying what I had written and mulling it over for a bit could I grasp the concept at hand.

Can one explain an idea one doesn't understand? I doubt it. These ideas were channeled through my mind but couldn't have originated there. I hasten to add, however, that once the ideas and their implications became clear to me, I always found that they fit in perfectly with what had gone before. In no case did I find contradictions.

As Storyteller told his tales in that expressive, melodious voice, I could hear him in my mind as though I were recalling a dear but long-lost memory. Several times I did more. The page before me would fade and I was no longer in my little cabin. I was beholding a scene in a Nanina hut group.

Dry brush had been piled beside the hearth of Storyteller and a boy of ten or so was feeding the fire to
keep it burning brightly.

The boy was his *arnak*, the one chosen as the next storyteller, for he must be trained to carry the traditions and genealogy to the next generation. Pine knot torches stuck into the ground stood burning like the footlights on a stage. Seated outside this circle were those who had come to hear the tales of Storyteller.

He strode within the circle, his long, brown hair unbound and flying about his head. Wearing only a loincloth, he told his tales, now crouching as low as the swoop of an owl, now leaping high into the air and flinging his arms to the heavens, spinning about as fast as the strike of a snake.

The flickering fire lit his face as it ran the gamut of emotions—love, sadness, tenderness, joy, disappointment—

his gesturing hands as expressive as his features.

The tales passed on to us are short and to the point, but he told many others which lasted an hour or more.

The audience was far from silent. Groaning in dismay or laughing in glee, clapping their hands in delight and gasping in wonder, they participated fully as the tales spun out.

Truly it was a memorable scene. I am sure I will never forget these glimpses of Storyteller at work.

As this book draws to an end, Storyteller's memory receded into the background and a mutual **knowing** took its place. I know not if I shall ever hear or see my dear friend again, but the gifts of knowledge and understanding he brought shall be cherished. My friend— my soul mate— I thank you with all my heart.

And now my task is done. Perhaps I should say my first task, for somehow I feel that others will be offered. In the interval I shall till my small homestead, tend my animals, and think on what has been given.

A GLOSSARY OF TERMS

arnak— Storyteller next in line of succession.

Babishta Hetchiyu— Bright Father, the sun.

chyan— Child. Usually used after a child's name, e.g.: *whishta chyan,*
Cloud Child.

curandero— A Mexican folk healer, usually using a combination of herbal medicine, faith healing and psychological counseling.

hei— A suffix denoting a physical or spiritual resemblance. (See *whishta hei*, cloud-like.)

Hetchiyu (see *Babishta Hetchiyu*)

Hiyasu— Mother. (See *Hiyei Hiyasu*.)

hiyasu kori— Night.

Hiyei Hiyasu— Mother of All.

horay— Separate, apart, lonesome. (The Nanina always assumed a verb was plural. *Horay* denotes the singular.)

horeste— Departing.

horeste, hiyasu kori— Leaving night.

hwashtay— Examine.

ishtahei— Like a stone; the people are one.

kora shay— Floating (in a spiritual sense).

korak— Disharmony between our physical and spiritual being.

kori— Time, in the sense of daytime, nighttime, blackberry time, etc. (See "horeste, hiyasu kori.")

nan— A person apart, a loner.

nan chyan parayi [accent is on second syllable]— Child dream.

nan chyan parayi [accent is on third syllable]— Child soul.

Nanina— A legendary golden-skinned people, renowned as spiritual teachers, who inhabited the Americas 3,000 years ago.

parayi— Dream. (See *nan chyan parayi*.)

parayi— Soul. (See *nan chyan parayi*.)

shay (see *kora shay*)

whishta chyan — Cloud child.

whishta hei— Cloud-like.

whishtan horay— Cloud apart.

wishtari [with the first syllable accented]— A feeling of happiness which wells up till it fills our being.

wishtari [with the third syllable accented]— An all-pervading joy.

INDEX

To order additional copies of
Way of the Spirit

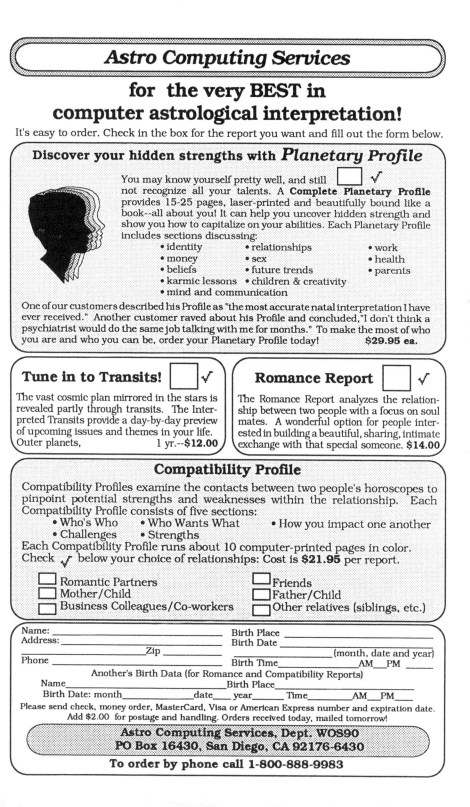